Managing a Quality System Using

BS/EN/ISO 9000

(formerly BS 5750)

Managing a Quality System Using BS/EN/ISO 9000

(formerly BS 5750)

PETER JACKSON *and* **DAVID ASHTON**

KOGAN PAGE

YOURS TO HAVE AND TO HOLD
BUT NOT TO COPY

First published in 1995

Kogan Page Limited
120 Pentonville Road
London N1 9JN

© Peter Jackson and David Ashton, 1995

British Library Cataloguing in Publication Data

A CIP record for this book is available from the British Library.

ISBN 0 7494 1443 X

Typeset by Kogan Page Ltd
Printed and bound in Great Britain by Biddles Ltd, Guildford and Kings Lynn

CONTENTS

5

PREFACE

Both of us are involved in quality systems, David Ashton as a consultant advising organisations on how to implement systems to meet ISO 9000, and Peter Jackson in managing a system. As a spin-off from working together on a quality system project, we wrote a book, *Implementing Quality Through BS 5750 (ISO 9000),* and have since written a second, shorter publication on broadly the same subject, *Achieving BS EN ISO 9000*, which takes account of the 1994 revision of ISO 9000/BS 5750. However, these books and others on the market, focus on setting up systems rather than managing them once they are implemented and we felt that here was a gap that needed filling. Our intention, therefore, has been to provide a practical guide to someone taking on the responsibility for managing a quality system. We hope it proves to be useful.

Peter Jackson
David Ashton

December 1994

1 INTRODUCTION

OVERVIEW

In the last few years almost all companies and organisations have had to recognise that quality matters – and matters more than almost anything else, because if customers are not given quality, if the products or services do not meet their requirements, they will simply go elsewhere. And with an increasingly global economy, there are few markets where customers cannot switch. To help in the quest for quality, there are a range of management tools to choose from. One approach that has become dramatically more common is quality assurance through implementing quality systems. This is very often coupled with assessment for ISO 9000 (still probably more familiar than BS 5750, but the same thing).

An organisation planning to introduce a quality system and be registered to ISO 9000 faces two tasks: designing and developing an appropriate system and, secondly, implementing and managing that system. The first task is a major project and will almost certainly involve the senior management of the organisation. There is also potentially quite a lot of assistance and guidance available: consultancy at all sorts of levels – some of it grant aided, seminars, other training resources and of course books (including two by the present authors). However, when it comes to implementing and managing quality systems there is rather less help available; there seems to be an assumption that a quality system will run itself. But this is just not true. A quality system has to be managed to a minimal level if it is to work at all, and managed with understanding and skill if it is to realise its full benefits.

As we discuss in later chapters, there are two sides to managing a quality system. The obvious one is taking care of the administrative routines that are built into a system – auditing, monitoring, corrective actions, management review, controlling the documentation, etc. All this must be done in a well organised way. However, once these routines are established and working well, they become rather mechanical and whilst calling for a certain attention to detail, some ability to organise and adequate record-keeping, the skills needed fall short of a full management role. However, there is another side to managing a quality system: the need to lead, to inspire and to motivate the organisation to use the system for real quality goals. The skills required here are less easy to define but they are very important and using them well is very much a true management role.

Quality system management, including these two sides to the role, can be organised in all sorts of ways, ranging from giving all the responsibility to one person (although with the support and participation of other managers) to sharing the work amongst a whole team and perhaps for- mally separating the administrative from the 'inspirational' elements. Each end of this spectrum, and all points in between, can work effectively. It all depends on the size, structure and culture of the organisation. Just for the purpose of writing this book, however, we have assumed that managing the quality system is the primary responsibility of one person – the quality manager and that he or she is working in a medium-sized organisation and that quite possibly being the quality manager is not a full-time job and the demands of this role have to be juggled with other responsibilities. We have also assumed that this manager comes into the job, with no previously relevant experience, at the point where a quality system has been designed but not yet implemented. There is, therefore, a need to get it all working, to train staff and arrange assessment to ISO 9000. The individual circumstances of readers may of course be rather different to these assumptions and, in this case, possibly some of the subjects will be less relevant than others. Still we hope that most of the material is of value and provides practical help to someone new to the quality manager's job.

THE STRUCTURE OF THE BOOK

Our intention has been to write a practical book, although more than just a description of the routines for the smooth operation of a quality system. On the assumption, however, that the reader is quite new to quality management generally, we start with some principles and theory. In Chapter 2 we discuss the concept of quality and its management and introduce the quality system approach. We also give an outline of ISO 9000, the recognised standard for quality assurance and against which most organisations developing a formal system will wish to be assessed. This discussion of principles is then extended (in Chapter 3) by looking at the potential benefits of a quality system. There are quite a few of these but it is unlikely that all of them will be equally important in any single organisation. However, we think it essential to understand what is being sought from a quality system and to regularly review whether these goals are being attained. One prerequisite for achieving any real benefit is commitment – commitment by the rest of the management team and commitment throughout the organisation. We stress the importance of this in Chapter 3 and return to the need for it throughout the rest of the book. For balance, we also consider in this chapter some potential downsides of quality systems; these need to be thought about to avoid common and serious mistakes in system implementation.

An overview of the role of the quality manager is provided in Chapter 4. This includes a summary of the tasks which are discussed in more detail in later chapters, but we also consider the skills and qualifications needed to be a successful quality manager and why the role calls for more than being an efficient clerk.

The remaining chapters slice up the quality manager's role and discuss it in relation to specific tasks and routines. Both an initial and ongoing aspect of a quality system is the need for staff to be trained in how to use it. This applies to all staff involved in operating the system (with few exceptions, virtually everyone) as well as those with specialist roles, including the internal auditors. These various aspects of training are covered in Chapter 5.

A quality system designed to meet ISO 9000 needs to be formal and documented. Moreover, this documentation needs to be well controlled. Chapter 6 discusses the quality manager's responsibilities in this respect.

Chapters 7 to 10 are all about monitoring the system in various ways: checking it works through internal auditing, continually monitoring the processes and the performance of suppliers and establishing whether customers are satisfied – customer satisfaction is what a quality system is all about.

However well designed, no quality system can avoid some problems and we discuss how these can be dealt with through corrective action (Chapter 11) which is also a tool in seeking continuous quality improvement. Numerical and statistical methods can assist in solving these problems as well as in monitoring the processes underlying the quality system but, potentially, statistics is a dry and forbidding subject to non-mathematicians. However, in Chapter 12 we hope to convince the reader that it does not have to involve much more than very basic numeracy and that even quite simple methods can be a really practical tool for the quality manager. The mechanisms for reviewing and changing the quality system – we argue that change is inevitable, desirable and ongoing – are then covered in Chapters 13 (management review) and 14 (changing a quality system). Choosing and working with assessors to gain ISO 9000 certification is the subject of Chapter 15 – again for the purposes of writing the book we have made an arbitrary assumption that beyond developing the system to meet ISO 9000 nothing has as yet been done about arranging for assessment.

In the last, short chapter we return to principles rather than giving practical advice. In this case we ask what comes next once the quality system is established. There does not have to be a next step of course, but our view is that a quality system that meets ISO 9000 is not a goal but part of a never ending search for quality.

QUALITY, QUALITY SYSTEMS AND ISO 9000

2

This chapter is about quality, how to get it, how to keep it and the relevance of ISO 9000. This background understanding of concepts and principles is required by anyone taking on the role of a quality manager. However, if it is all familiar ground – perhaps because you have already developed and implemented an ISO 9000 system – then please skim over the next few pages.

QUALITY – MEETING REQUIREMENTS

Quality managers are clearly supposed to seek quality, so what is this which is now of such central concern to businesses and other organisations? In everyday speech, quality is to do with the best, with excellence; it is some sort of absolute we strive for and perhaps a goal we can never quite attain. This sense of quality has some place in business but, day to day, it is not a very useful concept. Quality in the sense of excellence is often seen as the preserve of niche businesses – those at the top end of a market, supplying luxury goods to a few rich customers and not relevant to the mass producer or the business meeting a demand for satisfactory products at low prices.

Another concept of quality is simply that of meeting requirements and it is this which underlies quality management, quality systems and ISO 9000. Meeting requirements is particularly concerned with meeting customers' requirements since if we fail in this our business is doomed; customers will go to other suppliers who can meet their requirements. It is also not stretching the concept too far to apply it to public services which also, in the long run, must satisfy their customers and the taxpayer or eventually suffer the consequences – drastic change, abolition or perhaps privatisation.

Meeting customer requirements does not sound a particularly difficult thing to do – they want to be supplied with whatever they ask for and at a competitive price. If that is all quality is about why is so much written and said about it? However, these requirements are nearly always complex and often much more than what is specifically asked for.

The product alone, once we move from a simple commodity, is made up of many elements and features and often has to function effectively to meet the customer's own performance needs. There may also be expectations about reliability and how long it lasts. In the case of many consumer goods there are also intangible needs to be met through the branding and image promotion of the product: for example, the perceived associations of the clothes with some group or lifestyle is as much or more a real requirement as how it is stitched together. There are also the safety aspects of the product to consider – the customer may not mention ozone emissions of a photocopier but keeping within safe limits is a requirement which the supplier needs to think about (with possible legal penalties if this is not addressed). Requirements are, therefore, implicit as well as explicit.

Nor are requirements confined to product features. Too many manufacturing-orientated companies make this mistake. The service surrounding the delivery of the product is equally or more important. This covers short delivery periods or having the product in stock, keeping to schedules, providing associated paperwork including accurate billing and a back-up after-sales service, which is so important for any type of sophisticated equipment. There is also the matter of effective communication with customers, being able to respond positively to enquiries and deal with their problems. It is in these areas that very often customers are won or lost – service with a smile is the tritest of expressions but is always better than its opposite. Finally price and money is important in all markets. Of course we do not always want the cheapest but we seek some trade-off between valued features and price and the final choice is what we decide is best value for money. No supplier can ignore costs and pricing. Quality –

meeting requirements – at least cost is a vital component of successful businesses.

Quality is, therefore, a complex matter and concerns much more than technical product specifications. A commonly quoted definition of quality encapsulates this:

> The totality of features and characteristics of a product or service which bear upon its ability to satisfy stated or implied needs.

This understanding of quality applies to all activities including service as well as product orientated businesses and is equally relevant for all types of organisations including those outside the strictly business environment. Many public services are now committed to quality goals and quality management, and in some cases this takes the form of ISO 9000 registration. Also, the core focus of meeting customers' requirements can be effectively implemented throughout an organisation by recognising the concept of internal customers whose requirements have to be met as part of satisfying the final customer.

QUALITY MANAGEMENT

Few are going to argue that quality, in the sense discussed, is a vital concern. How, though, is this quality to be gained and kept? There are four broad approaches which we discuss below: quality inspection, quality control, quality assurance and total quality management (TQM), and these solutions to the quality issue were developed in this order. However, this does not mean that every organisation committed to effective quality management has or needs to go through the four stages in turn. Equally, in many organisations, all four approaches may be applied concurrently, perhaps in different areas. Also the later models of quality management built on the earlier ones and often incorporated their techniques – quality assurance almost always covers some elements of inspection.

Quality Inspection

Inspection focuses on the final product. In its purest form, the quality team works in the dispatch area rather than the 'factory' and its job is to compare the products coming out with some yardstick, a specification for the product, and this may incorporate a recognised standard applicable to the industry, eg a specific British Specification such as BS 1449 (for steel tubes). The work of inspection may be no more than simply looking at the product but more often will involve measurement and tests derived from the specification. Every final product may be inspected in this way, or, in the case of mass production, just samples selected from each batch. The outcome of inspection is that some – and hopefully most – products 'pass' and are sent off to the customer or into the warehouse, whilst any products not matching up to the specification (or more precisely outside the range of acceptable variation) are scrapped or returned to the factory for reworking. Scrap and waste are, therefore, the output of the quality team and high levels may suggest faults elsewhere but at least show the quality team are on the ball.

There are a number of problems associated with inspection, or at least with using inspection as the principal tool of quality management. One is that waste and scrap is institutionalised. The inspector's role ends with finding the faults and he or she has no responsibility for searching for the causes. Possibly no one else takes on the job either – it is just accepted that a significant proportion of resources have to be wasted on producing rubbish. And this waste is not just of materials which are often the lesser part of the loss. More costly may be the time of people and plant utilisation tied up in producing worthless output.

Another problem is that inspection and testing are not that easy and despite the sterling efforts of the inspection team, faulty products still go out to customers. Now the cost of rejects are still higher, including, quite possibly, a loss of a future stream of earnings because a customer is so dissatisfied with the faulty product.

But more fundamentally still, a quality management approach reliant on inspection can only address the product feature element of customer requirements. As we have discussed, however, there are many other aspects to quality, and whilst the product may be perfect, what about the delivery, other aspects of service and, for that matter, was it what the customer wanted anyway? Defining customer requirements is very much part of satisfying them.

Because of the narrow attention to product characteristics, it is not surprising that inspection, although well established in manufacturing businesses, is almost unknown in service activities. Here, there may be no physical product to test or the qualities may not be easily testable after the event. Also most service businesses recognise that they need to satisfy customers beyond simply delivering their core skills. Restaurateurs, for example, know that customers do not just want their hunger satisfied – the ambience provided, the presentation of the meals, the skills of the waiters and even how the menu appears are all part of a successful business. Where inspection has a role in service businesses it is often a matter of self-inspection by the practitioner – the chef, the solicitor, the doctor or consultant takes responsibility for maintaining his or her own standards and does not rely on an independent inspector to check out the work.

Returning to manufacturing, it is easy to poke fun at quality inspectors and their work – quality becomes a game of cowboys and indians (you decide which is which), although the failure that is implicit in this approach is not so funny. However, whatever its limitations, inspection of some sort is nearly always present in physical production and may be a regulatory requirement. Also, inspection is often incorporated into quality systems which are primarily built around quality assurance or even TQM concepts. ISO 9000, which is essentially a standard for quality assurance, requires an element of testing and inspection and related activities and this can lead to problems when applying the Standard to a service type business where independent inspection is unknown and alien.

Quality Control

As we discussed, a major limitation of the inspection approach is that the problems that lead to rejects and waste are never dealt with by the quality team whose role is restricted to the products rather than how they are made. The quality control approach seeks to overcome this by having the quality team not only identify defects but look for any causes in working methods, faulty machines, poorly trained staff, materials which are not to standard, etc. Also, inspection is perhaps brought into the factory with intermediate as well as final products tested. Such a quality control approach not only ensures that products are to specification (by inspection), but through going into the process, helps stop problems and waste arising in the first place. However, the quality control model, like an inspection regime, is limited to quality aspects which relate to physical parameters of the product and do not address all the other ways in which customer requirements need to be met.

Quality Assurance

Quality assurance – and this approach to quality management is the primary interest in this book – concerns itself with all activities with any bearing on meeting customer requirements. As well as the 'factory' the focus is on upstream activities such as establishing what the customer does want, design work in the widest sense and the procurement of outside resources, and also what happens after the product is produced. The latter includes storage and distribution and providing after-sales service. Inspection is often built into quality assurance (ISO 9000 demands this), and as in quality control, the causes of any defects found are investigated. However, a major strand of quality assurance is to take a more proactive approach and define 'best ways' – managing and controlling activities to obtain consistent levels of quality. There is also some emphasis on looking for long-term solutions to problems – in the terminology of ISO 9000, preventive as well as corrective action.

Quality assurance was developed in manufacturing initially to meet the needs of quality critical activities such as in the defence industries, but increasingly in all product-based businesses. More recently, and largely because of the importance attached to achieving ISO 9000, quality assurance has been applied to service activities, including, for example, professional services where there is no significant tangible product involved at all. Generally speaking, this approach to quality management can be effectively applied outside manufacturing. Any practical problems of implementation in service businesses usually relate, not to quality assurance as such, but to the earlier concepts of inspection and control, although in practice these are usually part of the whole approach, particularly where ISO 9000 is sought.

Total Quality Management

The fourth and (to date) final stage of quality management is TQM. This is a rather less defined and specific approach than the others and often involves motivation and fostering the right spirit rather than tangible and practical tools. Customers and their requirements are central and now there is perhaps a desire to go beyond merely 'satisfying' (a difficult enough job when the full implications are considered) to positively delighting them into ecstasies of joyful appreciation of the products and service provided. To be sure that this is being achieved, continuous customer monitoring is often one of the tools in a TQM package. TQM also seeks to dissolve all barriers to the goal of quality and delighting customers. Involvement and staff empowerment in quality activities – in the TQM perspective no activities are outside quality – are the means of ensuring this happens. Compared to quality assurance, TQM is far more people centred than systems orientated.

TQM, therefore, involves various techniques, and the consultants and gurus championing this form of quality management have put stress on different areas and specific techniques. Depending on where and how they are applied all of them can achieve impressive results. TQM is, however, very much part of the 1990s management vogue. In some cases, it may involve little more than lip-service to what is seen as the current fad. Obviously, in such cases, the output will reflect this half-hearted input. More deviously, the emphasis on staff involvement has also been seized by some as a new means of management control, a way of sugaring the bitter pills of downsizing, improving productivity and the other euphemisms for getting half the staff to do three times the work – another feature of the 1990s.

QUALITY SYSTEMS

Whichever approach to quality management is adopted, there needs to be some structure and organisation to the activities involved. There needs to be a system for quality management. In small companies this may well be informal with little or nothing written down. This can work effectively, especially where one person (the boss) is the real driver of the business. However, as the organisation grows or as we move up the scale of businesses, a more formal approach becomes necessary. With many more people involved, consistent quality management requires at least key instructions to be written down. Also, only a written system can be communicated to all staff uniformly and ensure that new employees know what is required to ensure quality standards are maintained. Typically such written systems grow haphazardly in a variety of forms until a point is reached where the whole thing needs tying together in some way. Often, it is only at this point that it is recognised that there is a quality system, although the formal manual which is created generally only codifies and standardises methods that were already well established.

A quality system, therefore, puts in place formal methods of quality management. These can be developed from scratch but as in most things, there is much to be said for applying established principles that are widely recognised to be effective. ISO 9000 is such set of principles – it is a recognised standard for quality systems and in particular a model for quality assurance.

ISO 9000

ISO 9000 is an international standard for quality assurance, recognised throughout the world. Nearly all countries also have their own national equivalent to the international standard and in the case of the UK this is not only equivalent but identical in content. Since mid- 1994, this British Standard has been designated as BS EN ISO 9000* but before then it was BS 5750 and it is still better known as this. BS 5750 was also the equivalent of and identical in content to ISO 9000 (and also to a European equivalent: EN 29000). In fact ISO 9000 was developed from BS 5750 (which originally came out of UK defence industry standards).

Before looking in any detail into the scope of ISO 9000, there are two potential sources of confusion about the Standard which it is worth clearing up. One is that ISO 9000 is a standard *for* quality systems and quality assurance and it is not a system which can be taken off the shelf and simply applied. It is applicable to any business or organisation and for this reason can only set out general principles to be applied and met. Implementation is through a unique quality system to meet the needs of a specific company and an effective application of ISO 9000 requires that considerable design time goes into its development. The second

---

* For simplicity, and because we are sceptical that BS EN ISO 9000 in full will ever pass into common usage, we shall refer consistently to the Standard as ISO 9000.

confusion arises from the fact that ISO 9000 is concerned with how quality is managed and does not directly address the quality of the output. By meeting the Standard and implementing an effective system a company will improve its capability to produce its products or service to consistent standards *whatever these standards are*. What standards are appropriate needs to be defined but certainly cannot be found within ISO 9000. In other words, ISO 9000 is not a product standard and claims that a product is 'made to ISO 9000' is literally nonsense. Two companies in the same business may both be registered to ISO 9000 but meet quite different product or technical standards. What ISO 9000 indicates is that both organisations have management systems in place to ensure that their respective quality standards are applied consistently and constantly.

ISO 9000 is set out in published form in a series of publications as indicated in Table 2.1. These publications fall into two groups: three models, indicated in Table 2.1 in bold typeface, and other guidance documents. The models define the Standard and anyone seeking registration to ISO 9000 must design a quality system to meet one (and only one) of these three models. The other documents provide guidance which may be found more or less useful in practical applications.

Table 2.1   The ISO 9000 series of standards

ISO reference	Subject
9000 – 1	Guidelines for selection and use of ISO 9000.
9000 – 2	Guidelines for application of ISO 9000.
9000 – 3	Guidelines for application of ISO 9001 to the development, supply and maintenance of software.
9000 – 4	Dependability management.
9001	**Model for quality assurance in design, development, production, installation and servicing.**
9002	**Model for quality assurance in production, installation and servicing.**
9003	**Model for quality assurance in final inspection and testing.**
9004 – 1	Guidelines for quality system elements.

9004 – 2	Guidelines for services.
9004 – 3	Processed materials.
9004 – 4	Quality improvements.
9004 – 5	Quality plans.
9004 – 6	Project management.
9004 – 7	Configuration management.

Anyone involved in managing a quality system to ISO 9000 needs to be familiar with the selected model – ISO 9001, ISO 9002 or ISO 9003 – and it is an implicit requirement of the Standard to at least have the relevant publication on file.

THE REQUIREMENTS OF ISO 9000 AND SELECTION OF A MODEL

The requirements of the ISO 9000 models are set out under a number of headings and these are listed in Table 2.2. In the case of ISO 9001 the requirements fall under twenty major headings and for ISO 9002 nineteen (ie nineteen of the twenty for ISO 9001) – the difference between ISO 9001 and 9002 is just the inclusion or exclusion of design activity. ISO 9003 includes only twelve of the requirements and is largely concerned with the inspection and testing approach to quality management rather than full quality assurance. Implementation of ISO 9003 rather than 9001 or 9002 is not common and will be ignored from here on.

In implementing ISO 9000 the choice of model (ISO 9001 or 9002), therefore, is usually related to the need to include design and in turn this depends on whether the business process involves activities of this sort. It is worth noting, though, that design can be thought of in a very general sense and be relevent wherever customer needs are in the form of general requirements and specifications rather than products. Design in this context, therefore, covers a very wide field including meeting clients' professional service needs (eg in solicitors), and is not just confined to the activities of specialised design teams producing drawings and prototypes as found in engineering. However, it also worth making the point that

Table 2.2 Requirements of ISO 9000 models

Reference	Requirement	Model 9001	9002	9003
4.1	Management responsibility	*	*	*
4.2	Quality system	*	*	*
4.3	Contract review	*	*	
4.4	Design control	*		
4.5	Document and data control	*	*	*
4.6	Purchasing	*	*	
4.7	Control of customer supplied product	*	*	
4.8	Product identification and traceability	*	*	*
4.9	Process control	*	*	
4.10	Inspection and testing	*	*	*
4.11	Control of inspection, measuring and test equipment	*	*	*
4.12	Inspection and test status	*	*	*
4.13	Control of nonconforming product	*	*	*
4.14	Corrective and preventive action	*	*	
4.15	Handling, storage, packaging, preservation and delivery	*	*	*
4.16	Control of quality records	*	*	*
4.17	Internal quality audits	*	*	
4.18	Training	*	*	*
4.19	Servicing	*	*	
4.20	Statistical techniques	*	*	*

ISO 9001 is usually only applied where design work is carried out as part of the service for a specific client – as part of the contract. Where standard products are developed and then marketed to a general market, ISO 9002 is the model usually applied (and of course also where no design work of any type is present). Far more companies are in fact registered to ISO 9002 than ISO 9001; the Standard's (ie ISO 9001) demanding requirements for design activities are undoubtably one factor in why this is the case.

Anyone developing or managing a quality system to ISO 9000 clearly must understand what is involved under each of the headings. However, it is not our intention to cover this in any detail in this book.* Other sources can be consulted, especially guidance and 'translation' documents written for specific industries – contact with an industry's own trade association will identify what is available in this respect. The requirements do, however, cover some activities which are particularly relevant to the quality manager's role and these will be mentioned briefly below and in more detail in subsequent chapters.

The title 'quality manager' is not actually used in ISO 9000 but there is a requirement for a member of the management team (such a status is explicitly required) to act as *management representative* (see clause 4.1.2.3 of the Standard). The specified duties of this manager are to ensure that the quality system matches up to the Standard as well as reporting on the working of the system to the rest of the management team. A note to the clause also deals with liaison with 'external parties' on matters affecting the quality system and in practice this usually amounts to dealing with assessors.

Some other aspects of the Standard which specifically relate to managing a quality system are set out opposite (the numbers and heading titles in italics are as per the Standard) but there are some difficulties in drawing a line since the whole thing is, of course, a standard for quality management and most or even all the requirements have some implications for the role of the quality manager.

---

* See Jackson and Ashton, *Implementing Quality Through BS 5750 (ISO 9000),* 1993, Kogan Page

ISO 9000 Requirements Relating to Management of a Quality System

■ *4.1 Management responsibility.* As well as the need for someone to act as 'management representative' this heading covers the need for a quality policy (which must be communicated effectively), defined responsibilities for tasks relating to the quality system, and providing the necessary skills and resources to ensure these tasks can be adequately carried out. There is also a need for 'management review' – a mechanism to ensure that senior management consider and make decisions relating to the system.

■ *4.2 Quality system.* The emphasis here is on a *documented* quality system with some minimum requirements to be met in this respect.

■ *4.5 Document and data control.* Not only must there be a documented system but this documentation must be controlled adequately so that everyone using the system works to common procedures. This may sound a trivial matter but in practice it is often a reason companies fail ISO 9000 assessments. Some positive management and administration is needed, especially in larger organisations where the number of copies of manuals etc can be considerable.

■ *4.14 Corrective and preventive action.* This provides the dynamic element to an ISO 9000 system and ensures problems are investigated and solved and, as a result, real improvements are made. It is not the quality manager's job to carry out the substantial work of corrective and preventive actions – investigating problems and proposing solutions – but it is his or her responsibility to make sure that these activities are carried out in a systematic and organised way and that any resulting action proposed and agreed is actually taken. These changes may involve revising the quality system and it is when changes of this sort are made (as they will have to and ought to be) that document control, as discussed above, can become problematical and require firm management.

■ *4.16 Control of quality records.* A quality system will produce records such as the results of inspection and testing. These need to be retained and filed so that they can be retrieved and used in actions to solve problems and improve quality. Planning and procedures are needed to ensure this happens. The records do not have to be in a paper form; computer files may be far more accessible.

■ *4.17 Internal quality audits.* A formal quality system simply will not work unless there is some audit mechanism. Auditing requires some special skills and needs to be planned and the quality manager has important responsibilities in this respect.

ASSESSMENT

Companies working to an ISO 9000 system invariably seek the recognition of formal assessment – being registered to the Standard by an accredited assessor body – and we conclude this chapter with a brief summary of what this involves (Chapter 15 goes into much more detail).

The major work leading up to assessment is to design an effective quality system – one which meets the requirements of ISO 9000, but more importantly, meets the needs of the individual organisation. That is why each system is unique. For most companies, developing such a system will be a major project and it is vital that someone has the responsibility of managing this work (but involving other staff as well). Very often, because no one else is available, the manager given this job succeeds to the functions of the quality manager and will, therefore, already have some good grasp of what is involved. However, for the purposes of this book, we will assume that this is not the case and that once the system is designed someone else has the task of implementation and ongoing management.

The system design task ends when the documented quality system is printed and ready to be used. In the subsequent implementation phase, the quality manager is very much involved, especially in the tasks outlined above including management review, auditing and corrective actions.

Once implemented and 'run in' for a reasonable period, the quality system can be assessed and the quality manager will certainly be involved closely with the assessment body. Quite possibly it will be he or she who selects a suitable assessor organisation for the work – there is now a wide choice of accredited bodies to choose from and the decision is in principle no different from choosing other suppliers of professional services.

The initial assessment is in two stages: a desk investigation to check that the documented system meets ISO 9000 and an on-site visit to find out if the system is actually being followed. If all is in order the certificate is awarded and that is that – for six months. The assessors then return because the process is not a one-off event but continuous with twice yearly surveillance visits and possibly periodic reassessment.

3   QUALITY SYSTEM BENEFITS

Managing a quality system and generally keeping it going requires a significant effort from the quality manager and other staff. Clearly benefits and a pay-off must be sought to make this effort worthwhile. As we shall show, there are a range of benefits which can be sought from a quality system and these will have greater or lesser importance in different organisations. Also, their importance may change over time and in particular the benefit which drove a company to implement a quality system and achieve ISO 9000 in the first place may become of less concern once the system has been running for some time.

The benefits sought should be an explicit goal and understood throughout the organisation and, as we discuss in Chapter 4, one of the quality manager's roles is to make sure this happens. Progress towards these goals should also be monitored and where possible measured. The quality manager also has a responsibility in this respect as well as communicating what such monitoring or measurement shows. The potential for formal monitoring and measurement is mentioned as the various benefits are discussed and also separately towards the end of this chapter. Further aspects of measurement are also discussed elsewhere, including in Chapter 12.

QUALITY AS THE GOAL

In a sense there is only one important benefit of a quality system which should be sought and that is quality itself; a quality system is justified if it significantly helps an organisation meet all the implicit or explicit requirements of its customers. Doing this will either bring its own rewards in terms of business growth or it will be a condition of survival – only those meeting the requirements will stay in the game in the long run. Meeting the requirements also has implications in terms of internal working and efficiency which is again bound up with the whole concept of quality. All this is of course true and every organisation needs to recognise and fully understand the need for quality and (the same thing) the need to meet its customers' requirements. However, left at this global level, the benefits and goals of the quality system are rather abstract and achievement is difficult to monitor or measure. Whilst, therefore, the overall quality goal should not be forgotten, it is more practical to focus on some of the more detailed benefits discussed below. Moreover, most, or arguably all of these benefits, relate to or are aspects of the global concept of quality.

MARKETING BENEFITS

If only in a negative sense, many companies implementing a quality system and ISO 9000 are seeking a marketing benefit – keeping business which they believe is otherwise at risk. In other words customers demand (or are believed to be likely to demand) that their suppliers demonstrate commitment to quality assurance through ISO 9000 and the company 'has to do it', like it or not. Less strong versions are where ISO 9000 becomes the norm in an industry (this can happen quite quickly) and a company without this standard starts to look odd and to lack commitment to quality.

The compulsion to have a quality system and ISO 9000 is a fact of business life although its degree is probably exaggerated. However, and more positively, a quality system can also offer marketing benefits where customers do not (or do not as yet) require their suppliers to be ISO 9000 registered. Having a formal quality system and being assessed to a recognised standard communicates a certain commitment to quality and, therefore, to meeting customer requirements. The standing and image of a company is as a result raised within its market and this may be particularly the case where ISO 9000 is still novel in the industry. (Any advantage of being such an ISO 9000 'pioneer' is, however, likely to be short-lived.) There is considerable anecdotal evidence, at least, that such marketing benefits of achieving ISO 9000 are real and lead to significant increases in business including opening up a new class of account that has previously been closed to the company. However, such marketing benefits will only be realised through marketing effort and by effectively communicating that the company has a quality system and ISO 9000. This activity is normally outside the role of the quality manager although he or she should ensure that the marketing team do not neglect the quality issue.

Whether positive marketing benefits are sought or whether gaining ISO 9000 is judged a commercial necessity, it is essential to ensure that the quality system is kept up to scratch and that registration is not lost (as it can be if the system is allowed to run down). The degree of marketing benefit or the necessity of achieving ISO 9000 may be debatable but it can do nothing but harm to lose registration. The quality manager has a primary role in preventing this sort of problem and at the very least he or she must ensure that the quality system is managed to at least some minimal level.

Monitoring or measuring the narrow marketing benefits of a quality system to ISO 9000 can involve logging when customers or potential customers raise the issue – eg as a formal condition of tendering or as part of their own supplier assessments – or through formal market research. However, it is very unlikely that the costs of the latter type of exercise could be justified if the survey's objective focuses just on the ISO 9000 issue; a more likely situation is where this is covered as part of a wider study of buyer requirements and buyer motivations. In any case, the management of market research will normally be well outside the quality manager's brief.

Whilst important, the gains from the marketing benefits of a quality system/ISO 9000 are likely to be short term. Having the certificate ensures the company can keep its key customers or allows it to reach a new qualitative level in its industry but generally speaking these gains are one-off and not cumulative. For this reason, whilst the marketing benefits may have been a sound reason for implementing a quality system to ISO

9000 in the first place, the drive for quality within the company will tend to run down if this is all that sustains it. At best the quality system will become just part of the corporate furniture and at worst something that is done with no point other than to keep the 'gong'. A quality manager inheriting this sort of situation needs to look for and champion other benefits from the system to give impetus and generate enthusiasm. More-over, these other areas offer real benefits and gains which might not be realised if the company is unable to lift its sights beyond having ISO 9000 just as a marketing tool.

MEETING CUSTOMER NEEDS

At the heart of an effective quality system is the desire to meet customer needs as fully as possible and various mechanisms built into the system help to ensure this is achieved. These include procedures related to the ISO 9000 requirements for 'contract review' (see clause 4.3 of ISO 9000), design review, verification and validation (clause 4.4), inspection and testing (clause 4.10) and the positive handling of customer complaints (through corrective and preventive action – clause 4.14). Meeting customer requirements also implies consistency – delivering the product or service to the same (required) standard every time. As already mentioned the link of a quality system to product or service standards is that it provides a means of applying the required standards both constantly and consistently.

Meeting customer requirements has to be a central concern of any business and brings its own rewards (or penalties if it is neglected). Arguably it is only another aspect of the marketing benefits of a quality system, perhaps the substantial part of marketing rather than the gloss of projecting a good image (in the long run image has to coincide with reality). However, there are further implications of meeting customer requirements which make it an even more important benefit. The opposite of meeting requirements is defective products or service which usually have to be corrected, reworked or scrapped. Therefore, a focus on meeting requirements is also a means of reducing operational problems. This is summed up in the maxim:

> *Getting it right first time, everytime.*

Because systems are in place to ensure effective working methods are followed, mistakes and defect rates are reduced. This aspect of quality system benefits will be picked up again shortly.

The quality manager's role in meeting customer requirements is first and foremost ensuring the system is working well and carrying out all the tasks implied by this. There is also a responsibility to make sure that all parts of an organisation recognise how crucial it is to meet customer requirements and, where it can be established, communicating evidence that this is being achieved. Such monitoring can include logging customer complaints and analysing their incidence over time (this is a requirement of ISO 9000). However, monitoring of this sort is really only concerned with gross dissatisfaction – by and large customers only start to complain when things are really going wrong. A more positive approach is to monitor customer satisfaction (rather than dissatisfaction) levels and possibly set formal goals in terms of raising a quantitative measure of this. The quality manager may be responsible for setting up and managing such a system or work with the marketing department. Some more detailed aspects of this subject are covered in Chapter 10.

EFFICIENCY

As already suggested, problem reduction and, therefore, improving efficiency can be thought of as an intrinsic aspect of meeting customer requirements. However, it is a sufficiently important benefit of a quality system to discuss in its own right.

In manufacturing, the key measure of this sort of efficiency is scrap levels and the result of a quality system can normally be demonstrated by falling reject rates, scrap levels and reworking. Often measurement systems for doing this are already in place before a full quality system is implemented and in this respect a before and after comparison may be possible. However, wasted material is only part of the cost of not meeting requirements in manufacturing. Often of more consequence is the labour cost and plant utilisation tied up in producing literally useless product. Measurement of this may be harder than of scrap material although some sort of standard costing linked to scrap levels will provide a reasonable approximation. Once we move into services, however, measurement of waste – which now may be wholly staff time – is usually far harder. Quite often no formal methods of allocation of time to tasks are in place, and even if they are, it is usually impractical to link time to unproductive 'waste' activities. Often, the only viable method available is to measure productivity – jobs completed per hour etc – and assume that improvements are linked to a reduction of inefficiency. However, the causal link may not be so simple and other effects of the quality system or quite different factors may make a significant contribution to apparent gains.

Such effects as reducing scrap rates are only one aspect of the efficiency benefits that may be sought from a quality system. Another is the effect of finding and putting in place 'best working' methods. These may be adopted for the first time on implementation of a quality system (or at least applied consistently for the first time) and the specific effects are likely to be very difficult to isolate in an overall before and after comparison. However, where new methods are introduced into an already established system, monitoring the results, if only qualitatively, ought to be under-taken – how else can you know that they are an improvement? Monitoring systems should, therefore, be part of the methodology of introducing new working methods into a quality system.

The quality manager has important roles in relation to obtaining efficiency benefits and these may include implementing changes to the system, putting in place effective monitoring of results and acting as a catalyst to encourage other staff both to identify positive changes and implement them effectively through using the quality system.

MANAGEMENT AND TEAMWORKING

Quality systems and ISO 9000 are usually thought of as concerned with impersonal issues and if anything to be positively people-unfriendly. However, this is a mistake and there are benefits to be sought in terms of a better management approach, and particularly through the wide partici-pation which should be part of an effective system. A good system requires such staff involvement at the implementation stage. If this is present when the system is set up, it can be built upon, particularly through the problem identification and solving mechanisms – auditing, corrective and preven-tive action and management review. In various ways, these should involve staff in investigating and proposing solutions to problems and a good quality manager will be concerned to bring in as much talent, from all levels, to carry out the work involved. In an effective system, staff should also be encouraged to look themselves for problems and initiate corrective and preventive actions. This is certainly a far more positive approach than using this procedure as a form of discipline and punishment. In other words, an effective quality system should be part of a problem-solving rather than a blaming culture. Fine-tuning the system so that this beneficial effect is achieved is also a responsibility of the quality manager.

A quality system is in many ways designed to stabilise – to ensure methods which are recognised to be effective are followed consistently. However, and paradoxically, a quality system is also an effective method of managing change through identifying the need for a different approach and, once validated, ensuring the improved working method is adopted and applied consistently. There is also a feedback mechanism (auditing) to make sure the change is effective. Quality systems are therefore a tool for managing change, the major challenge facing managers in a world where the pace of innovation appears to be ever quickening. The quality manager's responsibility in this respect is very much concerned with ensuring changes are effectively implemented and that the results are monitored.

A final aspect of the management benefits of a quality system can be summed up in the phrase 'due diligence'. Increasingly the consequences of product and service faults are customer claims, civil actions or the attention of regulatory authorities. We are not lawyers and certainly do not wish to make any categorical claims in this respect, but a management system designed to catch problems before they happen should at least reduce the chances of these sorts of problems arising and may provide grounds for resisting claims or actions – ie the defence that due diligence was exercised.

The methods of monitoring or measuring the management benefits of quality systems are in most cases embedded in the specific mechanisms, through recording, logging and evaluating results.

PROBLEMS WITH QUALITY SYSTEMS

In any decision to adopt a quality system – and a specifically ISO 9000 approach – the potential problems should be thought through and weighed against the expected benefits. From time to time the press emphasises (or exaggerates) the negative aspects of this management approach and it is not hard to draw up a theoretical debit list to set against potential gains. In some cases the balance may be against a formal quality system. However, an implicit assumption of this book is that the quality system is already in place and, therefore, there is little point, at this stage, to the pro and contra arguments to implementation. But there are some dangers in the operation of a quality system which should be recognised and which a good quality manager should try to minimise.

The biggest charge against ISO 9000 is bureaucracy. It is said that whatever benefits might be obtained, this sort of system leads to endless record-keeping and form-filling, often for its own sake rather than as a quality tool. It can be admitted that there is at least a nugget of truth here. Where assessment to ISO 9000 is sought, some record-keeping and even perhaps procedures really only have any point in relation to the assessors. However, taking the system as a whole, these requirements really require quite minimal effort. Nearly always serious excessive bureaucracy exists because the system was poorly designed in the first place. A quality manager doing his or her job properly should encourage nearly all such problems to be redesigned out of the system and an effective means of achieving this is an annual review of the record-keeping and forms built into the system. 'Is the record useful and is this the best way of keeping it?' should be asked periodically in relation to every procedure.

A linked potential problem is inflexibility. In the sense of ensuring adequate control and channelling initiatives effectively, procedures and systems are bound to have an element of inflexibility – the most flexible system is no system but in most cases the resulting chaos is unproductive. However, some sorts of inflexibility are a serious danger and should not be tolerated. In particular, a quality system is about helping a company to meet its customers' requirements and not putting up barriers to achieving this. Customers should never be told that their requirements cannot be met because 'procedures do not allow it'* even if this does appear to make for an easy life within the organisation. For example, to meet ISO 9000,

---

* An exception may be where meeting an expressed requirement is contrary to an accepted regulation, although arguably this would be a failure in meeting an implicit customer requirement.

contracts must be reviewed and the process documented. Some companies implementing the Standard have interpreted this to mean that customers must place orders in writing whether they want to or not. This is not so and may put in place just the sort of unnecessary barrier we mean. What may be required in this case is perhaps a method of confirming the order so that the customer can be sure that the product or service will meet requirements.

The quality system should be reviewed regularly, therefore, to ensure that such barriers to true quality are eliminated and not allowed to creep in. Clearly the quality manager has important responsibilities in this respect. Also the quality manager must check any tendency on his or her own part to favour procedures merely for administrative tidiness. A system should exist to ensure that customer requirements are met and this should always be central in the quality manager's thinking.

Quality systems are all very well but they must be followed. The basic rule in operating such a system is that if you do not like a procedure, have it changed, but in the meantime comply with it. In the initial enthusiasm for quality and a quality system, the need for long-term compliance is often put to the back of the mind, and particularly by those who are most creative in thinking up quality procedures. Also compliance can be a particular problem with senior management and this can have a serious knock-on effect to other staff – if the boss does not do it why should I? One way or another non-compliance needs to be tackled and the quality manager must see that this is done. However, it is better to shift any policing role to line managers – management of their staff is self-evidently their responsibility and the quality manager should in this respect be much more a facilitator than a doer. In the case of compliance problems from senior management, diplomacy and persuasion are more likely to be in order, although the potential problem here is an argument for making the quality manager appointment at a sufficiently senior level. This is discussed in the next chapter.

MEASURING THE BENEFITS

As the reader may have gathered by now, we are keen on measuring or otherwise monitoring things. In discussing the benefits of a quality system and ISO 9000 we have indicated some methods of measurement and in later chapters further details and more specific aspects will be covered. However, at this point there are two general issues to discuss.

Firstly there is the question of what should be measured and monitored since it is seldom practical or effective to attempt this across the board. Where it is benefits of the quality system which are being considered, the first thing to decide is which benefits are considered to be the primary goals of the system and organisation. We have suggested most of the possibilities but many organisations will rightly consider that only some of these have any importance to their own situation. Once this selection is made, then and only then, should thought can be given to the measures or more qualitative indicators which *in principle* can be best used to monitor the attainment of the goals. We then come to the question of which of these measures or indicators can be *practically* applied, bearing in mind the costs involved (see below). Quite possibly the ideal measure will prove to be impractical for one reason or another and a less precise or reliable one must be used instead.

An alternative but mistaken approach to selecting measures and indicators is choosing ones just because they can be easily and practically taken. The full logic of this is then to set goals on the basis that they can be easily monitored, which is obviously a nonsense. To select a measure solely because it is easy, is to act like the man who, joining a search for a valuable diamond pin lost in the park, concentrated his efforts on the bandstand platform. 'But I never went there,' said the lady who had lost the pin. 'Oh that's not the point,' said the man, 'it will be a lot easier to see it here.'

The second general point is that measurement and monitoring will always have a cost. This is true even where measurement is an intrinsic feature of a piece of equipment. While in this case taking the measurement has no marginal cost, taking readings of the measure and its interpretation will involve staff time. Such costs, and more usually also the cost of taking and recording the data, have to be weighed against any benefit from having the information. The crucial test here is to think through what decisions will actually be made on the basis of the data represented by the measurement. If these are likely to be inconsequential or might be made anyway, the measurement is unlikely to be worth its cost. Similarly, how big is the measurement cost likely to be in relation to the value of the benefit being sought – eg savings in wasted staff time? If the ratio is not significantly large it may be more sensible just to act on faith; in practice many quality or other management decisions have to be made in this way.

BENEFITS AND COMMITMENT

A final point to make in this chapter is that the achievement of any significant benefit from the quality system does require considerable commitment throughout the organisation, especially at the top. The board or the equivalent management group must take the matter seriously and communicate the importance attached to the quality issues throughout the company. This should be more than just a matter of the fine words of a well presented mission statement. Senior management must also be actively involved in practical quality issues arising from the system. The management review mechanism required by ISO 9000 is a start in this respect, although involvement needs to go further and take place in the day-to-day line management activities of directors (or equivalents). Just passing all the responsibility onto the quality manager will certainly not be acceptable. This point will be developed in the next chapter.

The need for commitment is also why systems created solely in response to customer demand are seldom satisfactory in the long run (or at least fail to realise many of the benefits that a quality system approach can bring). Because all that is recognised as important is gaining the ISO 9000 certificate, senior managers are unwilling to invest time in what is seen as a largely cosmetic exercise. But because that input is not there, the system will almost certainly be defective and limited. Where the original motivation was of this sort, it is far better to go back to basics, rethink the full potential benefits and if need be carry out a major redesign exercise. Part of the required change will be to put in the commitment that was missing first time round because the goals and horizons were too narrow.

4   THE ROLE OF THE QUALITY MANAGER

In the two previous chapters we have referred in passing to some of the responsibilities of a quality manager. This chapter covers the role of the quality manager in a more comprehensive way and provides an introduction to the many tasks involved in managing a quality system, the subject of most of the rest of the book.

THE NEED TO MANAGE A QUALITY SYSTEM

In the short term, a well designed system should run itself or, more accurately, be operated by staff without special management responsibilities for it. This is because nearly all the day-to-day activities required by the quality system procedures should be the responsibility of staff carrying out their 'normal' duties and work. The distribution department, for example, will have a number of procedures to follow and once trained in the system should not need continual overseeing in this respect. The same principle should apply in all the main functions covered by the system including agreeing contracts, design work, inspection and testing, purchasing, etc. However, this is the short-term situation and after some time entropy – the tendency for any system to become disorganised – will inevitably set in.

Manifestations of entropy in the quality system may include the following:

■ Defects in the system will not be corrected and as a result parts of the system will simply cease to work. This may reflect poor initial design or simply that the system has not been adapted to a changing environment.

■ The mechanisms for resolving quality problems will not be used effectively. These include identification of problems through auditing, corrective and preventive action and decision-making through management review. The consequence will be that one of the fundamental points of a quality system approach will be lost.

■ Compliance – following the system – will fall off, in the main because it will seem that nobody cares either way.

■ The senior management of the company will not know how the quality system is working and with other problems to address will not be concerned either.

The consequences of entropy in the quality system will be that it ceases to be effective and will eventually cease to produce any benefits (eg as discussed in the previous chapter). Eventually the run down will become evident to the assessment body during surveillance visits and keeping ISO 9000 registration will be jeopardised. To avoid these results of entropy and the associated problems, responsibilities for the management of the quality system need to be clearly defined and understood.

RESPONSIBILITY FOR MANAGING THE SYSTEM AND RESPONSIBILITY FOR THE SYSTEM

The problems discussed above can be prevented by assigning responsibilities for managing the quality system, and in all but really large organisations these will usually be shouldered by one person – the quality manager. However, it is essential to recognise that there is a distinction between responsibility for *managing* the system and responsibility *for the system*. As touched upon above, a quality system involves staff carrying out procedures in their normal work. The quality system is, therefore, owned by and the responsibility of the organisation as a whole and its success or failure cannot be offloaded onto the quality manager. But the 'organisation as a whole' is an abstraction and responsibility for the system must be recognised and taken on by all staff involved in the activities covered by the system. Above all, this must involve the organisation's senior management. If the system is failing to produce any real benefits, this problem should be a concern of the whole management team; the blame must not be simply put onto the quality manager. Quite possibly the root of the problem lies in how the system was designed and developed and, therefore, may pre-date the quality manager's personal involvement.

This separation of the responsibility for management of the system from responsibility for the system also sets limits to the role of a quality manager. The principle implies that even if he or she has the time available, the quality manager should not take on tasks which properly lie with line management and their staff. As we discussed in the first chapter, the whole point of quality assurance is to address quality issues at all significant stages of the process, and in nearly all cases this is best done by the staff involved in the processes. A good example of this is inspection and testing. As far as possible, staff should become their own 'quality policemen' and carry out checking work as an integral part of an operation. This is a better approach than the quality manager or his or her staff taking on inspection and testing. Problems identified in testing are more likely to be solved if the staff responsible are expected and able to solve them. Similarly purchasing evaluation should be left to the buying department, design work to designers (and other staff they need to consult in the process) and so on. All this is possible because the system prescribes standards which staff have to meet in their quality functions – having a team test its own output would be less acceptable if they were left to decide alone what tests should be carried out and how they should be done.

THE QUALITY MANAGER'S TASKS

Figure 4.1 summarises the quality manager's tasks and show how they all fit together. The tasks represented in the figure are the subject of all the remaining chapters in this book except for the last. Briefly, however, what is involved in each area is summarised below.

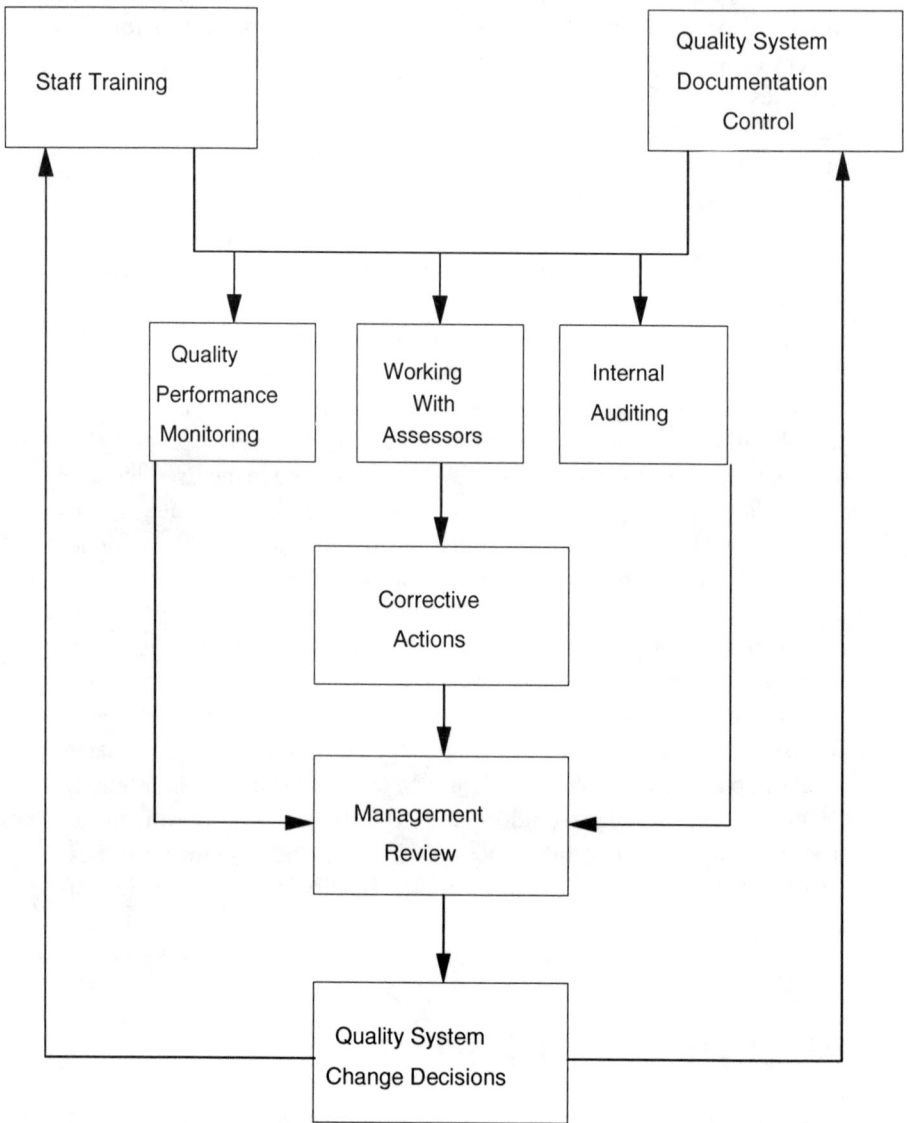

Figure 4.1 The quality manager's tasks

■ *Staff training.* All staff must have some training in the quality system and particularly in those parts which affect their day-to-day work. There are also some specialist roles – especially internal auditing – and training is needed for these tasks as well. The quality manager should be responsible for ensuring adequate training is carried out and may well personally lead some of the sessions. This subject is covered in detail in Chapter 5.

■ *Quality system documentation control.* An effective quality system depends on well controlled documentation. This includes the manuals which set out the written system but also associated documents such as equipment suppliers' manuals and the records produced through the operation of the system. The quality manager needs to ensure that all this material is kept up to date, in good order and above all is under control (see Chapter 6).

■ *Quality system performance monitoring.* The value of indicators of achievement of goals and benefits was introduced in the last chapter and the quality manager should at least be responsible for ensuring systems are in place to provide reliable data. As part of this approach or otherwise, there is also a need to monitor the performance of the processes carried out to provide a basis for planning improvements. The indicators involved may be simple or involve more elaborate statistical techniques and the quality manager should ensure adequate techniques are in place and applied properly (see Chapters 8, 9, 10 and 12).

■ *Working with assessors.* The quality manager will be responsible for working with assessors both to gain initial registration to ISO 9000 and to make the arrangements afterwards for continuing surveillance and possibly reassessment. This role also implies getting and keeping the system in a state where it is ready to be assessed and dealing with any follow-ups such as non-conformities which are raised in the process (see Chapter 15).

■ *Internal auditing.* No quality system will work without internal auditing. The quality manager should have the responsibility for ensuring staff are recruited and trained for this work, plan the work and implement any follow-ups required by audit findings. The quality manager, therefore, should head up the audit team (see Chapter 7).

■ *Corrective action procedures.* Internal auditing or performance monitoring will identify problems (non-conformities) which require solving. The corrective action procedure (this covers corrective and preventive action as per ISO 9000) provides a mechanism for investigating the cause of the problems and recommending solutions. Suggestions for improvement can also be filtered through this mechanism. Normally, the quality manager will not personally carry out corrective action investigations but he or she should ensure the procedure is followed and select staff for the *ad hoc* investigation work involved (see Chapter 11).

■ *Management review.* By definition, management review involves the whole management team. The quality manager's specific responsibilities are to ensure that this important process takes place, to present reports on various aspects of the quality system (including, as indicated in Figure 4.1, quality system performance monitoring, internal auditing and corrective actions), to keep records (minutes) and to ensure that any action agreed at the reviews is followed through (see Chapter 13).

■ *Quality system change decisions.* Management review decisions will often require changes to be made in either implementation of the system or in the actual procedures. In the former case there will be a loop back to training and in the latter to documentation (and probably to training as well). In either case the quality manager will be involved. Often, too, quality system procedures will give the quality manager some discretion to take action prior to referring the matter to management review, either where the matter is urgent or perhaps relatively trivial (see Chapter 14).

The tasks outlined cover all the specific requirements of ISO 9000 including those explicitly required and some that are implied or are logical extensions of a quality system to this Standard. (In later discussion we shall indicate where suggested activities are beyond what is strictly required for ISO 9000.)

From the tasks indicated it may appear that the quality manager's role is relatively mechanistic, administration rather than management. However, this is because the management rather than administrative role is implicit rather than explicit in many of the activities. Staff training, for example, is partly a matter of arranging suitable meetings, communicating technical knowledge and keeping a record of which staff have been covered in the training programme. This is necessary administration but the outcome will be very limited if the quality manager does not at the same time motivate staff, champion the value of the quality system approach and generally breathe life into the process. The quality manager also needs to take a positive and proactive role in management reviews – not just take the minutes. This sort of activity is the stuff of the management element of the quality manager's task. The implications of this dual role of administration and management will now be explored.

ADMINISTRATION AND MANAGEMENT

As we have indicated, the role of the quality manager requires both an administration and a management role. What is required in each case is different – the core skills of administration and management are compared in Table 4.1.

Table 4.1   Skills of quality system administration and management

Administration (system skills)	Management (people skills)
Planning	Leadership
Record-keeping	Championing
Reporting	Facilitating
Document production	Motivating
Liaison with assessors etc	Resourcing
Understanding of quality standards	

Administrative Skills

As already suggested the administration role is relatively mechanistic and is characterised by system skills. The need for these skills is obvious from the outline of the tasks required from a quality manager. Planning skills are needed in areas such as scheduling audits, arranging training, management review meetings, etc. Good record-keeping is needed in many of the activities carried out by the quality manager and there is also a need to ensure that records are kept adequately, by others, in other aspects of following the system. The quality manager prepares reports for management review meetings and for other reasons and some skills are needed in this respect. Document change and control requires the ability to draft and produce material. The quality manager will need to liaise with assessors and perhaps other third parties and although this involves some people skills what we really have in mind here is adequate correspondence standards and being able to make formal arrangements. Finally the quality manager needs to understand the requirements of quality standards and related matters (especially ISO 9000), and although this knowledge is supposed to be accessible to everyone, some find the quasi-legal aspect easier to handle than others.

Management Skills

These administrative skills are relatively well defined and where the question arises it should be possible, in most cases, to objectively assess whether a candidate for a quality manager's job has the necessary abilities. By contrast, the management skills are much more nebulous and although psychometric testing and similar techniques might be a useful aid in selection, assessment is by no means as clear-cut. The management skills are all to a large extent people skills – even resourcing, since what we have in mind is the ability to persuade senior managers to provide what is necessary. The boundaries between the skills are also vague and largely hang together since someone with an ability in one area is likely to be competent in the other. Briefly, the relationship of these skills to the quality manager's tasks is as follows:

- *Leadership*. Leadership is largely a matter of establishing the importance of the quality system and getting the rest of the company to act on this principle. Leadership needs to be applied throughout the system and company and will involve interaction with peers and superiors as well as staff of lower status. Defined authority makes the leadership task easier but it is not dependent on it. An effective leader can influence staff over whom he or she has no authority.
- *Championing*. In many ways this is similar to leadership. Championing means having a brief for the quality system and making sure its value and implications are considered throughout the company and particularly by peers and superiors – the senior management team.

- *Facilitating.* As already discussed, most day-to-day activities required by the quality system are carried out by staff in their normal work. The quality manager must ensure that staff are able to do this. In part this is a matter of communicating substantive information but it is also a matter of bringing groups together and acting as a catalyst to their self-development.
- *Motivating.* At its simplest this is ensuring most staff want to use the quality system. Stimulating participation and managing group dynamics are aspects of this skill.
- *Resourcing.* This has already been covered and is principally the ability, if need be, to fight for what is needed.

A difficulty of the need for a quality manager to have these two sets of skills is that few individuals have both of them equally. In fact they tend in practice to be mutually incompatible; not only is every child a little Liberal or Conservative, he or she is born a potential administrator or manager. Those with the good people skills may not have the attention to detail and delight in order which usually characterises the administrator but who in contrast often finds dealing with people a real trial. There is no perfect answer to this dilemma. One solution is to have two people split the role between them but this is seldom satisfactory since carrying out specific tasks may call for both sets of skills. Also, one of them needs to have overall responsibility but may tend to attach insufficient value to the role of the other. However, we contend that someone with the necessary people skills can probably carry out the administration to at least a satisfactory standard (perhaps delegating some of the work) but teaching a born administrator to be an effective manager is likely to be a more uphill struggle.

As we have already implied, we consider that the quality manager's tasks require one individual to have overall responsibility. Above a certain size of organisation this will amount to a more or less full-time job and as we move further up the size scale, the quality manager may head his or her own team. In small organisations, however, the quality manager role is still required but the individual concerned will probably also have other duties and have to juggle roles. Delegation of specific tasks may ease problems of being overstretched (this is true in larger organisations as well) but there will always be a juggling act involved.

THE QUALITY MANAGER AND SENIOR MANAGEMENT

As we have already argued, senior management has to carry the responsibility for the quality system and cannot simply offload its responsibilities onto the quality manager. Unfortunately this hands-off approach happens, particularly where companies implement a quality system simply to gain ISO 9000. The inevitable consequence is a system which produces little if any real benefit. Senior management has, therefore, a responsibility to be actively involved in the quality system both collectively (through management review) and in their individual line functions – taking responsibility for the system in the functional area they head up.

Because of the need to work closely and communicate with senior management and to be able to implement management decisions in relation to quality system matters, the quality manager needs to be part of the team responsible for the overall management of a company. ISO 9000 now (in the 1994 version) effectively requires this, ie in relation to the appointment of a 'management representative' (whose duties we regard as part of those of the quality manager's). In a small company the quality manager is likely to be a member of the board of directors or equivalent (and almost certainly will have other responsibilities). This status may be less necessary in a larger organisation but in this case the quality manager should be regarded as a senior member of staff and no more than one rung down from the board in the hierarchy. Also, in this case, he or she should answer directly to a board member, possibly to the chief executive.

Another reason for having a quality manager at a high level is so that he or she has sufficient authority to do the job effectively including securing resources and making sure that other staff give adequate attention and priority to quality issues and the quality system. This authority should be explicit and understood throughout the organisation. The chief executive or the management team as a whole should make this clear and give the quality manager both practical and moral support.

RESOURCES

Another facet of the quality manager's standing should be access to sufficient resources to do the job. This certainly includes money and there should be an agreed budget covering costs such as the salaries of any staff whose duties are largely related to the management of the quality system (likely only in companies above a certain size), assessment fees and stationery and similar physical supplies needed to operate the system. There is also the need to provide for training programmes whether these are largely in-house affairs or provided by outside specialists.

5 QUALITY SYSTEM TRAINING

There are a number of training aspects of a quality system and a quality manager has some responsibility in each case.

When the system is first implemented staff need to be motivated to use the system and periodically this may need to be reinforced. Similarly staff need to be trained in how to use the part of the quality system which most affects them in their day-to-day work – procedure training. Again this is required at the start-up of the system but some follow-up will be needed as well, particularly as the system changes. There is also a need to train new staff who start work with the organisation after the quality system is in place. Such induction training needs to include both motivational and procedure training. Operating a quality system also requires some specialist activities, particularly auditing, and good training in this area is very important to ensure an effective system. Finally there is the question of general training within the organisation – not in relation to the quality system tasks as such but training that enables staff to carry out their work effectively and in a general sense produce a high quality product or service.

All these aspects of training are covered or touched on in this chapter. As already indicated, for the purposes of this book, we have assumed that the quality manager is starting from the point when a quality system is designed and ready to be implemented.

RESPONSIBILITY OF THE QUALITY MANAGER FOR TRAINING

Before discussing training content and methods, it is useful to consider the formal responsibilities of a quality manager in this area since there will be an overlap with other managers and departments including, if it exists, personnel.

The major responsibility of the quality manager in relation to quality system related training is to ensure that it is carried out. How this is achieved is secondary. In a smaller organisation the quality manager is likely to be very directly involved and provide much of the training input. However, in larger organisations the quality manager will either need to or ought to involve other managers in the process and if there is a personnel or training department these staff should be better able to deliver the training than the quality manager. In this case the need is more a matter of agreeing the objectives and coverage of training programmes with the specialists. Similarly, it may be appropriate to bring in outside resources to provide training, although this is more relevant to auditor and other specialist training than more general needs, such as motivation and learning how to follow procedures.

An implicit requirement of any effective quality system and of ISO 9000 is management commitment to the system – a topic we have already mentioned. In training generally, it is essential that this commitment is effectively communicated. Even if for no other reason, therefore, some visible involvement in training by senior managers – especially the boss, however titled – is very desirable. We shall discuss this again shortly.

MOTIVATIONAL TRAINING

The objective of motivational training is to make staff *want* to use and follow the quality system. In other words, you have to sell the system to them. Unless this basic willingness is created, implementing the system effectively will be very difficult or impossible. If the process of designing the system was handled well, some of this motivation will have already been achieved, including through the involvement of staff in the development of procedures. However, we shall assume that this has not happened and that most staff, until now, have either known nothing about the new quality system or at most picked up a distorted picture through the rumour mill.

We discuss shortly methods of motivational training, but regardless of how it is achieved, the same subjects need to be covered. A suggested agenda is provided below.

MOTIVATIONAL TRAINING AGENDA

- **Introduction**
  - The organisation's unique quality system
  - ISO 9000
  - All staff involved
- **Why a quality system?**
  - The benefits
  - Well established approach (many other companies have ISO 9000)
  - Dealing with negative preconceptions
- **The documented system**
  - The main elements:
    - Quality policy
    - Quality manual
    - Procedure manual
  - The concept of controlled documentation
- **Procedures are mandatory**
  - The need to know and follow relevant procedures
  - But procedures can be changed
  - Controlled change
- **Change and quality improvement mechanisms**
  - Monitoring
  - Corrective actions
  - Management reviews
  - Not disciplinary devices
- **Auditing**
  - Why audits are carried out
  - The auditors' job
  - The audit team
- **Assessment**
  - Who are assessors?

> – How they work
> – Assessment timetable
> ■ Implementation arrangements
> – Timetable

In most cases what needs to be covered under each point of the agenda should be clear from reading other chapters in this book. In the paragraphs below our commentary is confined to only some of the issues.

Introduction

An important point to stress at the start of any motivational training session is that the quality system is unique to the organisation and has been carefully designed to meet its special needs. In other words it is not an inflexible, imported system to which the organisation has to adapt as best it can. On the contary, it should be stressed that ISO 9000 is a recognised international standard which the system meets but is not itself the system. In any motivational session this needs to be effectively communicated so that the system is rightly seen to be home grown.

Another principle to cover at the start of any motivational training session is that the quality system involves *everyone,* throughout the company. It is not of interest just to specialists such as the quality department (if this exists). One way or another all staff (or virtually all) will be required to use the system correctly.

Why a Quality System?

The key to effective motivation is to communicate the benefits, and these were covered in Chapter 3. As we discussed, all possible benefits will never apply to one organisation and it is important to be specific and focus on those which particularly apply to the company. Also, as far as possible, try and relate benefits to individual staff. A few rungs from the top of the company, overall company goals are inevitably rather abstract and it is better to link the benefits to day-to-day work. The wide uptake of quality assurance and ISO 9000 by all manner of organisations can also be covered, although there may be a downside to this. Possibly some staff will have picked up negative views about ISO 9000 from knowing someone in a firm that has implemented a quality system, or from the press. Such perceptions may need to be dealt with in motivational training or pre-empted. The best argument is along the lines that like most good things ISO 9000 can be badly implemented.

The Documented System

Staff need to be aware of how the system is documented (see Chapter 6 for a description of the documentation making up a system). However, not all documents are equally important to all staff; the quality manual is of rather specialised interest and most staff are unlikely ever to read it or need to do so. The procedure manual or manuals is of far greater day-to-day relevance, although most staff can realistically only be expected to be familiar with those procedures which affect their day-to-day work. Detailed discussion of procedures is best regarded as a separate task to system motivation and is discussed later in this chapter. The quality policy is, however, relevant to all staff and ought to be discussed in motivational training – not just the wording but what it means to staff in their everyday activities. An understanding of the policy, throughout the organisation, is a requirement of ISO 9000 and may be tested by assessors. However, this does not mean that staff have to be able to recite the policy like parrots; it is far better for them to be able to express the key points of the policy in their own words. But this presupposes they understand it in the first place.

In covering the documentation aspect of the quality system, the concept of controlled documentation should also be explained briefly with concrete examples of what this means, eg that procedures are not to be altered except in an approved and authorised way, uncontrolled versions of manuals are not to be used, etc.

Mandatory Procedures and Change Mechanisms

Motivating staff to follow the quality system willingly is important but the impression should not be given that compliance with the system is a voluntary matter – procedures have to be mandatory and this must be understood by all staff. Even so, it should be accepted that some procedures will prove to be ineffective or faulty and the need to follow procedures should be linked with the flexibility to make controlled change to the system. The specific change mechanisms of the system can be usefully briefly outlined. A related part of a quality system is corrective action and the positive aspect of this should be stressed; the corrective action procedure should not be seen as a disciplinary device.

Auditing

The detailed work of auditing will be carried out by specialists but all staff need to understand why this work is done, who the internal auditors are and how they will do their job. The limited role of auditors (eg not to blame staff, not to find solutions, etc – see Chapter 7) should be stressed. The assessment process should also be covered with an indication of how assessment will be carried out (see Chapter 15) when the time comes, and how staff will be involved.

Implementation Arrangements

The final area on the suggested agenda for motivational training is the timetable for implementing the quality system – when staff will be expected to follow the system and how problems such as work in progress at the time of start-up will be handled.

Carrying Out Motivational Training

The methods of carrying out motivational training and covering the suggested agenda are obviously very dependent on the organisation. A general principle, however, is interaction. The agenda may be covered in a formal style of presentation – kept, we suggest, to half an hour maximum – but an element of participation, discussion and question and answers should be also be built into the programme. The presentation element needs to be as professional as possible using good visual aids and this is where a training department will come into its own. The participation and discussion part, whilst open, free and frank, does need careful manage-ment to ensure that any negative feelings among staff are controlled. Above all any meeting must not become a general grousing session; the aim is positive motivation.

In a small company, the most effective method of communicating the motivational agenda is probably a general meeting of all staff. This helps to stress that the quality system involves everyone. The quality manager may lead the session but other managers ought to be involved and this probably requires a prior briefing session for them. The commitment of the whole company is best conveyed by giving a slot to the 'boss' at the beginning or perhaps summing up at the end. What he or she says is less important than visible and evident involvement.

As we move up the organisational scale, a general meeting becomes less practical and a number of sessions organised by department, section or site will be the only practical approach. Although different people may be involved in leading meetings and there may be different emphases and styles, some uniform and planned approach is desirable. Common visual aids and prior meetings of the session leaders are both means to achieve this. The commitment of senior management to the quality system must also be put across in larger organisations including if possible some involvement from the chief executive. If, because of the logistical prob-lems, a personal appearance is impractical, a video may be worth consid-ering.

PROCEDURE TRAINING

While in a small company, motivational training can be carried out at a general session, this approach is inappropriate when it comes to training staff in using procedures. This is far better done in small groups focusing on the specific procedures which affect the staff concerned. The only exception to this is training staff who, because of the nature of their job, will be involved with a wide range of procedures. Specialist staff such as auditors come into this category but their training is discussed separately and who we really have in mind is managers; the more senior the manager the greater the range of procedures which are relevant to their work. It is important not to neglect the training of this group, particularly if they are expected in turn to train their own staff.

Procedure training can usefully recap on some general principles covered in motivational training, especially that procedures are mandatory but changeable in an approved way. Document control is also worth emphasising again although this principle creates an immediate problem. Clearly access to procedures is essential in training sessions. However, while controlled copies of the procedure manual must be accessible to a department or working group, for reasons explained elsewhere (Chapter 6), a permanent copy for each member of staff cannot be recommended. But how can staff be trained in procedures without a copy of the relevant procedures in front of them? The only solution is often to make available uncontrolled copies for the purposes of the training meeting but to ensure that when the session ends all these copies are collected and removed – part of document control is to ensure that uncontrolled copies of procedures etc are not 'in use'.

Well designed procedures will be printed to a standard format and in the procedure training sessions the conventions used should be explained. Staff will then know how to read procedures effectively. The availability of the controlled copies should be discussed and staff encouraged to consult them when in doubt about the requirements of the quality system.

Arguably, well written procedures should not need to be explained in training sessions since they ought to be self-explanatory. However, it cannot be assumed that staff will actually sit down, read and comprehend procedures (this is as or more true of highly educated staff as of other employees). Therefore, in training sessions, each procedure should be discussed in detail until the leader considers that staff involved have grasped what is entailed. A danger in discussing procedures, however, is over-interpretation by the training leader. To elaborate on a procedure and read into it implications which are not explicit, is, in effect, to modify and change it. The result of this is that there is no longer a standard system; other staff may be following the same procedure but with a different interpretation.

Procedure training is obviously required when the quality system is first introduced. However, training is also likely to be required when the system is changed (as it will be). Without this extra input, staff are likely to follow the superseded procedures even though the controlled manuals have been amended. The required level of this sort of training is of course proportional to the degree of change; minor drafting corrections might be covered informally by an immediate manager but more substantial amendments may require a session comparable to the initial meeting.

Procedure training can be led either by the quality manager (or a deputy) or by immediate managers. In the latter case the trainers must themselves be given initial training and instructed in a common approach. Where one exists, the personnel or training department may also be involved.

Training staff in applying the quality system is a requirement of ISO 9000, and for assessment purposes it is recommended that a record is kept of the training given in procedures. This need not be elaborate or any real burden; a brief outline of the content of the training (perhaps copies of or reference to any material used), the date of the course and a list of participants is adequate. The same principle of keeping records also applies to the other aspects of training covered in this chapter.

INDUCTION TRAINING

Probably all organisations which are serious about their quality system (and why have one if they are not?) will arrange, at least minimally, adequate initial training when the system is implemented. Quite often, however, the training phase is then assumed to be complete and no attempt is made to introduce new staff to the quality system as they join. It seems to be assumed that they will just pick it all up through osmosis.

New staff must be formally inducted into the quality system with broadly the same ground covered as in the initial training sessions and this includes both procedure and motivational training. Procedure training of new staff is probably best done by line managers but there should be some formal structure to this, perhaps set out in an induction checklist. The motivational part is rather harder to organise for staff starting a few at a time. Depending on the numbers involved, a short session led by the quality manager might be organised every month or quarter.

Training in the quality system is only part of induction. For new staff to be rapidly effective, all round induction is essential. However, this is straying into areas of general and personnel management well beyond the scope of this book.

SPECIALIST QUALITY SYSTEM TRAINING

One specialist training need is of course that of the quality manager. Outside training courses can of course be considered and may be a good investment. However, we hope that reading this book from cover to cover will give a newly appointed quality manager at least a sound grounding in his or her new role and, for this reason, we do not pursue this aspect of specialist training any further.

The quality manager apart, the key specialists whose training needs to be considered are the internal auditors. Auditing and trained auditors are essential to an effective quality system and good training here will always pay off. ISO 9000 requires that auditors are trained for their work but does not specify how this should be done. In a small organisation, working to a tight budget, self-help auditor training is quite feasible and may involve little more than the newly appointed quality manager and the audit team discussing together the principles of auditing and what is required in practice. Chapter 7 is about internal auditing and provides a starting point for such self-learning. If a consultant was involved in developing the system he or she may also assist in informal training.

However, while self-help is possible it is less than ideal and carries the danger that, with a poorly trained team, auditing will not be as effective as it needs to be. Wherever possible, therefore, external training should be considered even if only for just one of the team – he or she can then cascade the course contents to the others (not forgetting the quality manager who effectively leads the audit team).

There is no shortage of auditing courses available, ranging from one-day seminars upwards, and these can be either external or in-house (only economical with sufficient numbers of trainees). There are recognised standards and qualifications in auditor training and the bottom rung is to become a Registered Internal Auditor. This involves attending a two-day course, its syllabus and leader approved by the IQA,* and subsequently completing a number of internal audits. Training to this recognised standard is well worth considering – other, unrecognised,

---

* IQA – Institute of Quality Assurance: PO Box 712, Southwalk Street, London, SE1 ISB. Tel: 0171-401 2988. The IQA's publication *Quality World* is also a useful source for quality related training courses and other matters.

courses, such as one-day seminars, may be satisfactory but there is no assurance of this. The IQA also approve courses leading to more advanced qualifications – Registered Assessor and Registered Lead Assessor – but these are way beyond the needs of small and medium-sized organisations.

Auditors need to be very familiar with all aspects of the quality system, especially the procedures. In planning auditor training, therefore, time needs to be set aside for this and obviously it can only be carried out in-house; outside training is no use here. Various approaches can be used including discussion meetings of the quality manager and audit team, backed by thorough reading of the documentation.

GENERAL TRAINING

The final area of training to consider is general training in the skills required to do the work of the organisation and this potentially applies in all areas and at all levels – from the chief executive to office junior. Such training is a requirement of ISO 9000 (see *4.18 Training*) and includes both identifying training needs and arranging for their provision. In reality, little is needed to meet the letter (but not the spirit) of this requirement. A manager who simply records on a list of staff that each has no training need (after, of course, deep and careful consideration) is possibly doing sufficient to satisfy the Standard and assessors. However, this is to miss the point.

Training and staff development is clearly a precondition of real quality and never more so than today. With the current pace of technical and commercial change, no staff are truly competent for more than a short period after they initially qualify and ongoing and continuous staff development is essential for an organisation to succeed. This is true whether or not a quality system is implemented and ISO 9000 sought. A quality system does, however, provide some framework around which to build continuous and effective staff development with (in the Standard) a dual requirement to identify needs and ensure these are met.

Aspects of identifying training and development needs include some mechanism for considering the overall skill needs of the organisation and this is likely to be an offshoot of the general business planning process. The next step is some sort of skills audit. This will involve all managers and some discussions with staff. The latter approach then leads to asking what training and development staff themselves are seeking. Such meetings can be very informal in a small organisation but inevitably need to be rather more structured in a larger operation and may sensibly be integrated into an appraisal system.

Once needs are identified, the resources to provide them have to be put in place. In part this is a matter of money – a training budget – but also required is management time to ensure staff receive the training they require. If there is a personnel department, they will take on some of this work but line managers also need to be involved. Nor should this be considered an extra duty – staff development is a key role of any manager.

One problem with training is that often only paid-for external courses are regarded as the real thing by both staff and managers. However, in most organisations, a lot of effective training is on the job and possibly informal. All that may be needed here, to integrate this into a formal training process, is some simple record system. Keeping records of external or other 'classroom' training is also a part of a more formal approach and a requirement of ISO 9000. On top of training, there is staff development to consider as well. The boundaries here are vague, but development is probably more self-initiated and may be no more than reading around a subject – perhaps the trade press. Such initiatives should, however, be encouraged and recognised by management.

An organisation taking the ISO 9000 training requirement seriously may wish to consider the Investors In People scheme. This goes further than required for ISO 9000, although most of the documentation needed for Investors In People is likely to be in place through the quality system. Details of this scheme can be obtained from a local Training and Enterprise Council (TEC), who should in any case be approached for advice, help and possibly assistance on all training matters, including those linked to the quality system.

The specific role of the quality manager in general training will vary greatly between different organisations. Where a personnel or training function exists, much of the planning work will be handled by them and the quality manager's involvement may be no more than ensuring an adequate linkage into the quality system. Where such a facility is not present, the quality manager is likely to take on more responsibility, including ensuring records are kept of training needs, assessments and of training completed. Other managers will, however, have to be involved, not least because otherwise all the quality manager's time will be taken over by this important function.

6   QUALITY SYSTEM DOCUMENTATION

A quality system has to be documented and looking after the manuals, records and other parts of a system is an important responsibility of a quality manager. This chapter discusses various aspects of this work.

As in other chapters, we assume that the system is already designed, but we briefly review the various elements which make up the system. The very important concept of document control is then discussed as well as some practical ways in which control can be kept. Bound up with control is the need for staff to have access to copies of system documents and some of the implications of this are discussed. The final topic covered in this chapter is keeping quality records.

THE PARTS OF THE SYSTEM

ISO 9000 requires that a quality system should be documented and specifically refers to a need for a quality policy, quality manual and documented procedures. Quality plans and works instructions are also mentioned though not in a way which indicates that these are always required. Figure 6.1 represents in pyramid form these parts of a docu-mented system, together with the quality records produced through oper-ating the system. The document layers higher up are more general (and shorter) than those shown nearer the base.

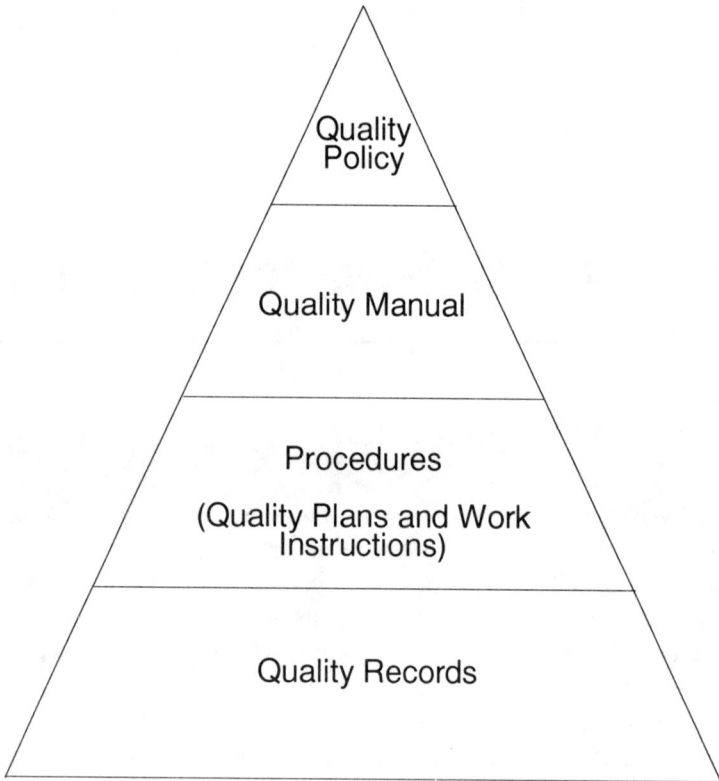

Figure 6.1   The quality system pyramid

It is assumed that the quality system is already designed and that, therefore, these documents have been prepared. However, it is still useful to discuss the role and format of each one. The terminology of ISO 9000 is used for the documents but this does not have to be the case – each can be called something different (eg guide to the quality system instead of quality manual and working methods instead of procedures) if this is preferred, providing that the terms are defined somewhere in the system (eg in the quality manual) and related to those used in the Standard.

Quality Policy

The quality policy should be a very short document which defines an organisation's policy for and commitment to quality. It can be expressed in all sorts of ways although ISO 9000 has requirements (see heading *4.1.1 Quality policy*) for what should be covered:

ISO 9000 Requirements For A Quality Policy

- Quality objectives and commitment
- Link to the organisation's wider goals
- Link to customer needs and expectations

A policy statement will also usually refer to the quality system as a whole and the standard (ie ISO 9001 or ISO 9002) met. All this can be expressed in less than a page and any longer is too long-winded. The policy needs to be communicated throughout the organisation and we shall discuss the practical implications of this shortly.

Quality Manual

A quality manual is a formal requirement of ISO 9000 (see heading *4.2.1 Quality system: general*). The key purpose of this part of the system is to describe how the requirements of ISO 9000 are met in the quality system as a whole and provide cross references to other parts of the system – especially to the procedures. The following extract from a quality manual illustrates what we mean in relation to just one of the major headings of the Standard – a similar approach is required for all the ISO 9000 headings. The numbering and headings in italics are as per the Standard and cross references are given to corresponding procedures.

    4.14   Corrective And Preventive Action
       4.14.1 General
       Problems arising from the processes carried out or from the operation of the Quality System, whether identified by audit or other staff or through customer complaint, shall be investi-

> gated, analysed and corrective and preventive actions recommended and authorised through formal Procedures (see Procedures 11.4). These procedures also cover the documentation of corrective actions.
>
> *4.14.2 Corrective Action*
>
> *4.14.3 Preventive Action*
>
> The distinction between corrective and preventive action is recognised but the Procedures use 'corrective action' to cover both requirements.

This sort of formal description of the quality system and how it relates to the Standard is of particular value to outside assessors and enables them to easily relate the system to the standard against which it is being audited. In addition, however, it is also an important guidance document to the quality manager and the internal auditing team, particularly when changes to the system are being made or considered. As will be discussed in a later chapter, changes to a system are both possible and necessary but the quality manager has a responsibility to ensure that the modified system will still meet the requirements of the Standard.

The description of the system in relation to the Standard, in the form outlined, forms the major part of a quality manual. Other contents are likely to include:

- a brief background to the organisation and a description of its structure;
- the quality policy (whether or not this is also available as a stand-alone document it is usually also bound in as part of the quality manual);
- a statement of the scope of the system – the major documents making up the system (eg procedures as well as the manual), the standard met (eg ISO 9001) and which parts of the organisation are covered by the system (all of it or defined parts).

Again much of this is for the benefit of outsiders and particularly assessors.

Procedures

Day to day, for most staff, procedures are the quality system – they describe in practical, actionable terms what needs to be done to comply with the quality system. Documented procedures are a formal requirement of ISO 9000 (see *4.2.2 Quality system procedures* – the need for procedures is also mentioned in most other headings as well). In developing the system, most of the time and effort will almost certainly have gone into procedure drafting and the wider the range of staff involved in this work, the better and the more effective the procedures are likely to be. As time goes on, procedures will need to be changed and the quality manager will be involved in redrafting them.

We recommend four principles of effective procedures to guide amendment or a review of existing procedures:

- understandable;
- actionable;
- auditable;
- mandatory.

Procedures are to be followed and, therefore, they must be understandable – and understandable by the staff who are to follow them. The ability of staff to read and understand instructions will vary through an organisation and it is recommended that procedures should be drafted with the least able reader in mind – they should, therefore, use the simplest language, short sentences and avoid dense blocks of text.

It may seem obvious that procedures should be actionable but it is quite easy to write high sounding ones which cannot be followed in practice – perhaps the conditions assumed are not present or another step in the process does not happen in the way implied. Even with the greatest care, a complete system written from scratch will almost certainly contain in early versions procedures which are not actionable and the first amendments made to a system are likely to be correcting mistakes of this sort.

Procedures should also be auditable. In other words there should be some evidence *after the event* that the procedure has been followed (or not). This is not simply a matter of making life easy for the internal auditors. If a procedure cannot be audited it is no more than an expression of good intentions. So why have it there at all? Setting out intentions is not the purpose of procedures.

The final principle is that procedures are mandatory. Any staff involved in the process covered by the procedure, must follow that procedure. If the procedure is not effective (or could just be better) then the system should be changed, but until this is done, staff should be expected to follow the procedures as best they can. By extension, it is recommended to leave out of procedures the possibility that a procedure need not be followed or is semi-optional. Phrases such as 'it is preferable' or 'it is good practice wherever possible' are better omitted.

All the quality system procedures can be bound together (a loose leaf form is best to allow amendment) and all staff given access to the complete set – to the procedure manual as it is often called. An alternative approach is for departments to have available just those procedures which are relevant to their own work and this may be the better approach in a larger organisation; if nothing else the procedure set used by a member of staff will not be such a forbidding looking tome. However, document control (discussed shortly) is probably harder with this approach.

Quality Plans and Work Instructions

Although referred to in ISO 9000, neither of these parts of a quality system are a definite requirement and many organisations will choose not to include one or both of these types of document in their own systems.

While quality plans are not a requirement of the Standard, quality *planning* – a management process – is. Quality planning is how a quality policy is translated into action and covers issues such as developing and implementing effective procedures, providing adequate resources which affect quality (eg manufacturing and inspection and measuring equipment) and training staff. The process of planning should also ensure that the quality policy is followed in each piece of work carried out for a customer including in unusual projects. Documentary evidence is required that effective quality planning is undertaken but often this may take the form of other parts of the system – especially in procedures or perhaps in business plans or the minutes of management meetings. However, where a major change in working methods is planned (eg installing a new type of process machine) or an unusual order is to be met (eg a very large order or one requiring working methods which do not match standard procedures etc) it may be appropriate to prepare a formal quality plan which relates the planned activity to the quality system and policy. Quality plans of this sort may also be specified in the contract with the customer. This type of document is, therefore, usually very specific in contrast to procedures which relate to a broad range of operations. Therefore, each plan is likely to be an *ad hoc* document but one which includes some cross references to general procedures.

A quality plan, if required, should be prepared by staff involved in the activities covered by the plan and a special team may need to be gathered to draw it up. The quality manager will be involved in this work, perhaps convening the meetings, possibly chairing them and very likely drafting the plans. Once prepared and agreed, the plans need to be available to staff involved in the work covered by the plan, and positive steps may be needed to make sure that if plans are amended, it is the latest version which is used.

If quality plans are for special projects, work instructions are for standard activities. A typical example is where a company produces a range of products or services and a set of works instructions is produced for each one – they are particular 'recipes'. Works instructions can also be thought of as detailed procedures and in any case should be linked and cross referenced to the relevant procedures. Works instructions are by no means relevant in all systems but can be an effective method of controlling production and achieving consistency of output – a major aim of quality management. They may be developed as part of related procedures or added afterwards, in which case the quality manager should be involved in drafting them or vetting others' work to ensure a uniform format.

Quality Records

Quality records are created through operating a quality system and the procedures (possibly also quality plans and works instructions) will determine their format and whose responsibility it is to produce them. Where the records are to be kept by using specially designed forms, these need to be linked to the relevent procedures (eg by a numbering system) and it is common practice to attach copies of the forms at the end of related procedures. This subject is also covered at the end of this chapter.

DOCUMENT CONTROL

The principle of document control and its practical application is of the greatest importance in any quality system. It is an explicit requirement of

ISO 9000 and a common reason for failing initial assessment. Moreover, the whole concept of a quality system approach requires this sort of control. Although all staff need to understand document control, the quality manager has a special responsibility to ensure that this is maintained effectively.

The objective of document control is to ensure that all staff follow the same quality system and work from the same manuals etc. If this is not the case there is clearly not a uniform system in use. Uniformity is a fundamental of the whole approach. The need for control is also linked to changes in the system. When a quality system is new, all staff are likely to use the same documents because different and later versions do not as yet exist but once the system is changed there is a real danger that some staff will follow the new version while others, not aware of the change, stick to the superseded version. At its simplest, document control involves ensuring that all staff use only controlled copies which are all identical and the latest version. No other copies of manuals, procedures, etc, should be 'in use'* within the organisation.

We can recommend several techniques for keeping quality system documents under control:

- *Visual distinction.* It helps if controlled documents are visually distinctive; everyone then knows that they are controlled and that they should not be altered except in approved ways. There are various ways of achieving this including using special paper (eg with a border) or having 'controlled document' in faint print. A cheaper alternative is simply to stamp each page 'controlled' after it has been printed.
- *Version numbering.* As a system develops, new versions will replace old versions and control is very much easier if each page of controlled documents shows the current version number and perhaps date of issue. Whether this is the latest number can be checked against a master copy or a document list (see below). Where a document is more than one page (a manual or set of procedures) it is also good practice to show on each page, not only the page number but the total

---

* In Chapter 5 we mentioned some practical problems in relation to training and suggested that temporary 'uncontrolled' copies are made available in this case but then withdrawn – they are not, therefore, 'in use'. Nor are file copies of superseded documents retained as a record of any changes made.

number in the set, eg '1/3' indicates that this is the first page of a three-page document. For reference purposes, procedures at least also need to have a numbering system (eg 1.0 Design Procedures).

- *Master copy.* The quality manager should hold an up-to-date master copy of every controlled document making up the system. There is then a measure of what is correct.

- *Controlled document list.* Similarly there should be a list of all controlled documents by number and title showing the latest version number and date of issue. The documents listed should be to the level at which change is made or anticipated to be made. This might be the whole quality manual since this document is likely neither to be very long nor often changed, but the change level for procedures will more conveniently be linked sets such as those affecting one process or activity. In this way, a change in one detailed procedure need not involve changing the whole procedure manual. The master list should be kept by the quality manager but copies may also be attached to all sets of documents (and of course updated as the list is amended when new versions are issued).

- *Circulation list.* Control of documents implies a finite number of copies and a list is required showing where each is kept and who is responsible for its safekeeping (eg the department manager). Each set of documents can be numbered to match the list (copy number one etc). Where complete sets of procedures are not given to each department (ie they have only those most relevant to their normal work) the list needs to be rather more complicated with some form of matrix of documents and keepers. Organisations working from more than one site also need more elaborate methods of control in this respect.

- *Document inspection.* Despite all these practical techniques of control, the quality manager should carry out or organise inspection to ensure that only up-to-date and controlled documents are actually in use. This can be carried out as a special task or made part of the audit procedure (see the next chapter). If a problem is found, something needs to be done about it and if possible it should be prevented from happening again, ie the corrective action procedure should be used (see Chapter 11).

- *Training.* Lastly staff need to be trained in the concept and importance of document control and the practical steps required to ensure this is kept up – see the previous chapter.

Any forms used as part of the quality system must also be controlled to ensure the up-to-date versions are used – forms are as or more likely to be revised as any part of the procedures. Copies of the forms are typically bound with the procedures to which they relate but separate copies are used for record-keeping and the quality manager needs to ensure that these are correct and up to date. To avoid confusion with other forms, which are not formally part of the quality system, it is useful to print copies on a special colour of paper (not used for anything else). Version numbers are also needed on forms and some numbering system relating each to the relevant procedure is to be recommended.

As well as material specially written and printed, quality systems often incorporate as part of the procedures 'outside' documents. A good example is an instruction manual for a process machine; rather than specially write up all the details of operating it, the procedures for the relevant department simply refer to the manufacturer's own operating manual. Similarly, industry codes of practice may determine how a particular task is carried out and again the procedure may just refer to the relevant document. This is a sensible approach but such documents, since they effectively form part of the quality system, need to be controlled.

Where there is only one or two copies and they are not regularly updated (eg suppliers' manuals) control of outside documents may be fairly easy to ensure although as an addendum to the circulation list the quality manager should keep a list of each such document and possibly uniquely identify each copy. Rather more difficult to control are the likes of industry codes where multiple copies come into the organisation by various routes (possibly including those addressed to the homes of staff who are members of a relevant body). As a minimum, the quality manager should ensure that up-to-date, labelled copies of such documents are held and that staff are instructed to check whether any other copy they intend to use matches the file copy. Incidentally, an up-to-date copy of ISO 9001 or 9002 is part of the system and should be held by the quality manager and updated if new versions are published (as in 1994).

As mentioned earlier, a critical aspect of document control is to ensure that only controlled copies of quality system documents are in use within the organisation. Sometimes it is appropriate to pass copies of these documents to outsiders; the quality manual, for example, may be given to potential customers and some procedures may be given to subcontractors to make sure their work matches up to requirements (it would be unusual to pass copies of all procedures outside the organisation and more common to regard them as internally confidential). Any documents passed outside the organisation cease, by definition, to be controlled and each copy should be accordingly labelled as such (or at least not labelled as controlled).

ACCESS TO DOCUMENTS

Control is easy to ensure if all quality system documentation is kept under lock and key by the quality manager. However, this defeats the point of the documents; they are a guide to action, so how can they be followed if staff do not have easy access to those which are relevant to their day-to-day work? It is hard enough getting staff to read up procedures etc without putting barriers in their way. However, it is unfortunately true that there is some conflict between control and access. The more copies and, therefore, the more accessible they are, the harder it is to keep them under control.

The access needed varies between the different parts of the quality system:

- *Quality policy.* All staff need to be aware of and understand the quality system and this is helped by making copies widely available – one given to each member of staff, copies displayed on walls, etc. Copies may also be used for marketing purposes. Because it is part of the quality system, control of policy statements is needed and this becomes an issue if it is decided to change it – whether this is because the organisation wishes to do so or for other reasons.*
- *Quality manual.* Relatively few staff are likely to need regular access to the quality manual although it should be available if requested. Copies held by the quality manager, auditors and perhaps an open-access 'library' copy may be sufficient.

---

* For example, most organisations with a pre-1994 quality system would probably need to revise their quality policy to take account of the retitling of the Standard in that year, from BS 5750 to BS EN ISO 9000.

- *Procedures.* The trade-off between access and control is most apparent with procedures. All staff need ready access to the procedure manual or at least those procedures that affect their day-to-day work. However, one copy per person or even one copy per senior person is too many to exercise practical control and a better approach is one copy per department or working group. This copy needs to be kept in an identified place, which is accessible to every member of staff needing to use it. In the department manager's locked filing cabinet will not do. Removal of the copy from this point should be discouraged even to the point of a locked bible approach although there is always a danger that it then becomes such a holy object that nobody dares to touch it. Getting the balance right is not easy.
- *Quality plans.* These will typically concern a project team and each may need a copy with the master held by the quality manager. If amended, new versions should be issued and old ones discarded – document control also applies to this part of the quality system if it is in use.
- *Work instructions.* Copies need to be available to each member of staff involved in the processes covered. Within one department there may be more copies of these instructions than the related procedures and they should be as near the point of use as possible. They may be printed on hard or laminated card so that they withstand regular use. Again document control principles should apply.
- *Record forms.* In carrying out many procedures, records will be needed to demonstrate that they have been correctly followed in a particular case or to record readings associated with a particular procedure (eg process operating temperatures). These records are often kept by completing relevant forms although this does not have to be the case – sometimes 'freehand' records are just as practical or the data may be kept as computer files (see below). Where forms are in use, adequate copies need to be available as near to the point of use as possible and the quality manager and line managers need to ensure that the arrangements for doing this are adequate and systematic. There is also a document control need which becomes a practical issue if the forms are amended – the old versions need removing and new ones brought into use and this needs organising – it cannot be left to chance. In theory, copies of forms can be made, by the department

concerned, from those bound with related procedures but this is not a good approach. Unless a positive distribution system is set up, new version copies may not be brought into use. Furthermore, the procedure manual or sets are likely to be left in disorder with pages left out – control then breaks down.

QUALITY RECORDS

The completed forms etc form the quality records and the need for these and looking after them is specified in the Standard (the need to make records is mentioned under most of the headings and keeping them comes under *4.16 Control of quality records*). Quality system procedures will, in each case, specify the form in which records are to be made and who is responsible for ensuring that this is done.

Quality records are often seen as a negative and bureaucratic element of ISO 9000. In this view, records are kept just because the Standard and the assessors demand it or to make the work of auditors possible. However, this is a wrong and negative view. Records are needed not only to demonstrate that the system is being followed but also to provide data which can be used to identify and help solve real quality issues. Dealing with customer complaints and even product liability claims is also much easier with adequate record-keeping. Moreover, while ISO 9000 may indicate where some records are needed, there is considerable latitude to ensure that only those really critical to process quality are kept. Also the form of record-keeping is for each organisation to select, to ensure the minimum cost and time is spent on recording. Much of the record-keeping will pre-date the quality system – even organisations without a formal system keep many records – and the real difference is likely to be that the approach is better thought out and the quality and completeness of the records much higher. Unnecessary records are a bad thing, but time spent keeping poor and incomplete records is even worse.

The effort that goes into record-keeping should, therefore, be balanced against the value of the data. However, this presupposes that the records are kept in such a way that they can be used effectively. The relevant heading of ISO 9000 (*4.16*) requires that a framework for this should be set out in procedures (either a specialised procedure or embedded in the procedures which give rise to the records). These procedures need to cover how records are to be identified (eg linked to product identification), collected, filed and indexed, stored (this could be near the point they are produced or centrally, perhaps collated by project number) and how long they are to be kept (and what happens then). The practical arrangements covered by these procedures, or needed to implement them, will vary considerably. The quality manager has a responsibility to ensure that all this works effectively through practical involvement and ensuring that record-keeping is covered in internal audits. Some records will be produced through tasks carried out or controlled by the quality manager (eg audits, corrective action, document control, etc) and he or she needs to ensure that these are kept in good order if for no other reason than to encourage others.

Different records are likely to need different retention periods and the nature of the product or service may also be a relevant factor. If for no other consideration, all records will need to be kept for at least a year to meet the needs of outside assessment. Retention periods need to be specified in procedures, as does what is to be done with them at the end of this time (eg secure disposal).

Keeping paper records for any time generates a considerable archive for which secure space must be found. Also the greater this volume the harder it will become to find a particular record, and useful retrieval is a prime requirement of an effective system. For these and other reasons many companies will want to consider keeping records as computer files with all the advantages this brings in terms of space saving and, above all, instant and selective access. Some of the records may also be generated automatically through the operation of a computer-controlled process.

Computer records will be particularly attractive where the hardware and other infrastructure is already in place, especially networked systems. The Standard specifically allows for this form of record-keeping and on-screen access to data is sufficient; there is no need to produce hard copy of all data routinely. However, the records must be secure and this certainly means back-up to media such as discs or tape and possibly off-site storage of key data to allow post-disaster recovery.

A computerised approach can also be considered as a means of making procedures and other parts of the documentation widely available. If the file can only be amended through restrictive access, this will overcome many of the problems of document control (by definition all users in a network will see the same up-to-date version).

The practical side of computerisation is beyond the scope of this book and is likely to be a major project in its own right. Proprietary software for quality system record-keeping is now available from many suppliers.

7 INTERNAL AUDITING

Internal auditing is a vital part of a quality system and ensuring that this work is carried out is one of the key responsibilities of a quality manager. This chapter discusses the objectives of auditing and why audits have to be carried out. The selection of an audit team and the process followed in auditing is also covered. Finally, some practical guidance on how to carry out an audit is provided.

AUDITING OBJECTIVES

The objectives of auditing are to answer three fundamental questions about a quality system.

1. Does the quality system meet the Standard?
2. Is the quality system being followed?
3. Is the quality system making an effective and efficient contribution to the organisation's goals?

It is assumed in this book that any quality system has been developed to meet a standard – ISO 9000 – and it needs to be established that the match exists. Of course, the assessment process will provide a final test of this and any serious omission in the design of the system is likely to be identified at the desk investigation stage of assessment (see Chapter 15).

However, it is better to be confident of the match well before this point is reached, or it may be found that a quite radical overhaul of the system is required after it otherwise appears to be functioning well. Even after successful assessment, the question of meeting the Standard remains since both the system and the Standard may change. Changes in the system will be required for internal reasons – so that it works better, to correspond with changes in operations and to improve working methods – but there is a possibility that the revision may no longer match the Standard. Similarly the Standard itself is revised from time to time (the last change was in 1994) and each time this happens at least some change is likely to be needed in a quality system, even if it is largely cosmetic.

The internal audit team – including the quality manager – of a small- or medium-sized organisation is unlikely to feel qualified to determine whether or not a system matches up to the Standard, at least not when it is first implemented. The quality manager may well be the chief architect of the system (ie he or she led the project that developed it) and, therefore, on theoretical and practical grounds, needs someone else to review whether or not the system is to the Standard. In practice, therefore, other sources are usually relied on to answer the first question of the auditing objectives. In the period between implementation and first assessment, a consultant may be used for this purpose or the assessment body may be asked to carry out a pre-assessment audit. Either of these costs money of course, but are likely to be less expensive and disruptive than failing the assessment because the system does not meet the Standard. In the case of changes to the Standard, the assessment body used will probably give adequate advice on how the quality system needs to be revised. Fundamental changes to the quality system to meet the internal needs of the organisation are in practice unlikely to be needed for some time after it is first implemented and by this time the quality manager and the audit team may well feel confident to review the revisions against the Standard and be able to make a reasonable judgement. However, one principle of auditing is independence (see below) and arguably the quality manager cannot audit a change in the system which he or she is closely involved in making and some independent source should be considered, even if it is little more than informal advice.

The second question – is the quality system being followed? – is the objective which is most often met by internal auditing. Often this process is thought of as a process of seeking out problems, policing the system and generally finding fault but this is at least the wrong emphasis and certainly a counter-productive way of presenting the audit role within the organisation. The outcome of audits may well be that problems and deficiencies are identified and these may relate to people problems but the initial approach ought to be positive – is the system working? – rather than negative – what is going wrong here? This distinction may be subtle, but getting it right strongly effects the success of the overall audit process.

Where problems and deficiencies are identified, these are recorded and as we shall discuss later may lead into a corrective action procedure. However, it is important to understand that the auditors' job ends at identifying the problem and the solution is found by someone else, outside the audit process. If an auditor confuses problem identification and solving he or she ceases to be independent – the vital qualification for an auditor. Where auditors are full time (only likely to be found in large organisations) this separation between problem identification and solving is fairly easy to achieve. More difficult is where auditing is a part-time role and in other work the auditors are involved in finding solutions to problems. To overcome this, part of auditor training must be to learn how to wear the audit hat and the necessity to separate out other roles while doing so. This distinction between problem identification and problem-solving applies to auditing in its widest sense and not just in relation to establishing whether or not the system is being followed.

The final question relating to the effectiveness or efficiency of the system is often not considered in audit work yet to omit it entirely is to miss the whole point of the quality system. Unless the system is just there to gain ISO 9000 – a very poor reason for having it – it should be achieving benefits such as quality improvements, efficiency savings, enhanced customer satisfaction and the other things discussed in Chapter 3. The auditors' concern in this case is not to make a judgement on whether the level of efficiency attained has improved and similar issues, but to establish whether anything is actually being done to achieve these goals. Their specific role in this context is, therefore, firstly to check whether monitoring activities related to the effectiveness of the system are being carried out (as defined in the procedures, quality plans or otherwise) and secondly to audit whether the results of such monitoring are being translated into positive action through corrective actions and management reviews.

WHY INTERNAL AUDITING IS REQUIRED

Although gaining ISO 9000 should not be the only reason for having a quality system, it is usually a major goal of the whole project. Internal auditing is a formal requirement of ISO 9000 and, therefore, if for no other reason it will need to be carried out. The Standard sets the requirements for internal auditing under heading *4.17 Internal quality audits* and this requires that a system should include procedures for auditing.* Internal auditing also has a linkage to assessment since done well, the process mirrors most of what the assessors will do during the on-site initial assessment or later surveillance visits (see Chapter 15). Internal auditing, therefore, prepares an organisation and its staff for assessment and, furthermore, should identify problems before the assessor. If at assessment any major problems that are found are a surprise to the quality manager, the internal auditing has been poorly done. Another aspect of the link to assessment is that one of the first things the assessor does on a visit is look at the internal audit records and if these suggest auditing is inadequate this will be regarded as an indication that the whole system is probably not working (also, of course, inadequate auditing is itself a deficiency in assessment, since it is a failure to meet one of the Standard's requirements).

Meeting ISO 9000 is, therefore, one strong reason for internal auditing. However, we believe that there should be other reasons for doing quality related things apart from gaining the certificate and there are other strong arguments for effective auditing. One such reason is that, without auditing, the organisation's management cannot be sure that the quality system is working well. In fact we can be more definite than this – we can be confident that some part of the system will *not* be working but we cannot be sure which part and, therefore, nothing can or will be done to put the matter right. Without any corrective action taken, such problems will tend to grow rather than diminish and will spread to other parts of the system. For one thing staff will notice that no steps are taken to identify problems and will take this as a lack of management interest. Why should they care either? In the long run (and this may not be very long) an unaudited system

---

* There is also a separate standard for auditing – BS 7229/ISO 10011 (in three parts) – and this is worth at least a look.

will simply run down and none of the benefits sought will be realised. Moreover, all the work that went into developing the quality system will be wasted. Internal auditing is, therefore, essential for the working of a quality system and for this reason alone it is a vital activity.

Auditing is also a step in achieving the quality improvements which ought to be one of the benefits sought from a quality system. As we stated earlier, auditing itself should not propose solutions to problems and, therefore, does not directly find more quality-effective ways of doing things. However, auditing initiates a process which leads to improvement and this is represented in the quality triangle shown in Figure 7.1.

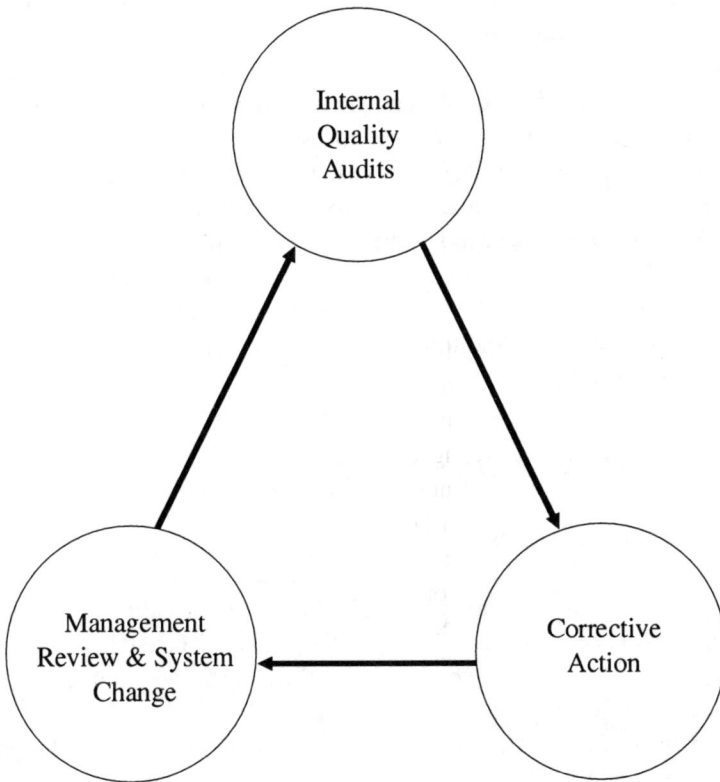

Figure 7.1 The quality triangle

Audits identify problems, including those whose solution would lead to a quality improvement. A separate process of corrective action then produces a proposed solution and a decision to implement this is taken though management review. This may include a change to the quality system to include procedures which (it is hoped) will lead to enhanced quality. Eventually, auditing is repeated, to check that the solution is effective and if it is not, the triangle is followed again and, if necessary, again until the problem is solved. Later chapters will discuss the other activities in the triangle but for the moment it is enough to understand that this very effective mechanism relies on auditing to set it in motion.

Finally, auditing assists staff development and this also leads to improvement in the performance of the organisation. Provided it is done in the right way, the questioning of routine practice helps staff responsible for the area being audited to take stock and perhaps a fresh look at how they carry out the work. An objective review of working practices should lead to the questioning of those practices, even if the system is being followed, and encourage staff to suggest improvements in working methods. Also, since auditors are outsiders to the departments they audit (they must be if the audit is to be independent), they broaden their own horizons and take this wider view back into their own working areas (assuming they are not specialist, full-time auditors such as might be found in the largest organisations). Auditing, therefore, improves internal communication and opens up an organisation.

SELECTING AN AUDIT TEAM

If the quality manager takes on the role when a quality system is first implemented, an immediate task is to select and train an audit team. There are two formal requirements specified in ISO 9000 that auditors must meet and they also need some personal qualities as well. The quality manager needs to understand these when selecting the team as well as deciding its size and the input required.

The two formal requirements of an internal audit team are that they are independent and that they are adequately trained. Training was covered earlier (see Chapter 5) and will not be considered further here.

Independent means independent of the area being audited – an auditor cannot audit a part of the organisation or the quality system which they are themselves involved in day to day. Apart from any danger that identified problems might be ignored out of regard for the team of which the auditor is a member, problems and deficiencies will probably not even be identified since the 'wrong' method will be regarded as the usual or correct way of working. In practice, auditor independence can be achieved in two ways: selecting auditors from areas not covered by the quality system and cross auditing.

ISO 9000 and most quality systems do not cover all the operations and areas of an organisation. Accounts and finance are the most common exclusions but there are often others as well. Staff from these areas can, therefore, after training, audit with appropriate independence, the parts of the operation which are within the system. Similarly, specialist audit staff carrying out no other work are also independent but this is only likely to be a realistic option in a very large organisation unless their employment is part time or on a consultancy basis. These methods of achieving auditor independence have much to recommend them. Because the team is usually quite small (compared to the case with cross auditing) training can be in-depth and not too expensive. The team also builds up experience since they will be auditing frequently. Another advantage is that, because they are not involved in operating any part of the quality system, they can be more objective in outlook. However, this detachment is often the problem with this approach to independence; the auditors are seen as, or are, remote, ivory towered and unrealistic in their approach to the quality system. At the worst they become over-legalistic in outlook.

Cross auditing consists of training staff involved in the main operations of the organisation to carry out audits in departments and areas where they are not involved – eg staff from purchasing audit the production area and vice versa. A strong case for this approach is that it increases involvement in the quality system and, through exposing staff to new areas, opens up the organisation and stimulates fresh ways of looking at operations. However, such an audit team is likely to be larger than one of specialists and consequently more expensive to train (since they carry out fewer audits it will take longer to gain the linked experience as well) and more difficult to manage. Also, cross auditors may find it harder to be objective – they may tend to be sympathetic to staff 'too busy to follow the quality system'.

A final point about independence is that since auditing is itself part of the quality system, it should be included in the audit schedule (the same applies to the quality manager's work). However, how can auditors independently audit the process since they are directly involved in it? There is no complete answer to this. For a variety of purposes, the audit team should periodically meet and review their work and the best that can be hoped is that self-criticism and 'standing back' is encouraged.

Prior to any auditor training, there are no formal qualifications required for audit work. A knowledge of the processes carried out in the areas to be audited is useful but not essential. A reasonable level of education, literacy and the ability to communicate verbally and in writing is required, but the most important personal qualities of auditors which should be considered in recruiting the team are human relations skills. How the auditors get along with other staff and how they approach the work will influence how effective they are. Specific skills in this respect which should be sought include the ability to effectively present themselves and their task to other staff, the ability and tact to deal with 'difficult' and perhaps more senior staff, patience, a certain tenacity so as not to be easily fobbed off with an evasion and a cooperative rather than authoritarian approach. Auditors also need an attention to detail; an audit should consider what is precisely required by the system – it is not enough to establish that it is more or less working. Arguably, audits should be carried out to the point of 'nit picking' but not in a way that makes staff over-defensive. Reasonable neatness in work is useful too and goes with attention to detail. The point of these qualities should be apparent from the later discussion of what the auditor actually does in an audit.

Bearing in mind both the formal and personal qualifications of auditors, the quality manager can select a team. A difficult problem at the start is knowing how big the team should be. The formal answer to this is that it should allow the audit schedule to be carried out successfully bearing in mind the size, complexity and scope of the organisation. However, what this schedule may entail and what input will be needed to complete it may not be clear when the system is first implemented. Another consideration is how much time each auditor can make available to this task, assuming they are not full-time specialists. There is also a need to cover for absences. When starting a team from scratch, the best approach is usually to train up just a few (possibly only one or two) auditors and after some experience expand the team as necessary. As a very rough and ready guide, an organisation with 50 –100 staff based at one site may require, to do the job well, an audit input of three man-days per month.

THE QUALITY MANAGER AND AUDIT TEAM

The quality manager should head up the audit function and be responsible for the recruitment, training and review of the audit team. He or she needs to prepare the audit schedule, initiate and assign audit tasks (see below) to ensure the schedule is met, receive and consider the audit reports and keep adequate records of the work. There is also a need for the quality manager to see that action is taken as a result of audits including, where appropriate, the corrective action procedures and follow-up audits. Some or most of these tasks can of course be delegated – eg to the leading auditor or record-keeping to a secretary – although the quality manager should retain overall responsibility. In most small- to medium-sized organisations, however, the opportunity for such delegation is likely to be quite limited.

The quality manager's auditing responsibilities may therefore be summarised as follows:

- audit team:
  - recruitment;
  - training;
  - review;
- audit scheduling;
- assignment of audits;
- receive and consider audit reports;
- keep audit records;
- initiate or monitor follow-up action.

As head of the team, the quality manager should fully understand audit work and probably gain some hands-on experience. However, unless shortage of staff makes it inevitable, it is usually better for the quality manager not to carry out routine audits. One reason for this is that at least a partially objective view can be taken of auditing performance. Also, deciding on what action to take after an audit is better done with a certain detachment.

THE AUDIT PROCESS

A typical audit process is represented in Figure 7.2 – although the basics are common for all quality systems, the details can vary. The process should be set out in a formal written procedure (a requirement of ISO 9000). Although this can vary widely in style and detailed contents, all the elements in Figure 7.2 should be covered one way or another. Each step in the process is discussed below.

Audit Schedule

Audits need to be planned to ensure each part of the system and its implementation is covered at least once a year. In a small company it is usually enough just to base the schedule on covering groups of procedures (with all the procedures covered over the year) since there is generally a correspondence between departments or areas of the operation and pro-cedures – each set of procedures mainly applies to one functional area only. Another approach is to schedule on the basis of departments/areas and in each audit to cover the procedures which apply in that particular case. In larger organisations, however, with common procedures applying across departments or sites, the schedule needs to be based on a matrix of procedures and departments or sites as illustrated in Figure 7.3. The aim should be to cover all areas and all procedures over the year but not necessarily all procedures at all sites. The size and degree of complexity of the organisation will determine how many auditors and auditor-hours are needed to complete the annual schedule.

The schedule should be prepared by, or in consultation with, the quality manager at the beginning of the year (probably with a date for this specified in the audit procedures) and 'published' – this may simply be a matter of giving a copy to each auditor and/or displaying it on a notice board. The quality manager should retain and file the master copy. This schedule should be a real plan and a realistic guide to the audit work that is actually carried out. However, it should not be inflexible – if there is an urgent need to audit an area or set of procedures out of schedule, then this should be done. Customer complaints, a rise in rejects or comments from staff may be grounds for doing this. Schedules can also build in this

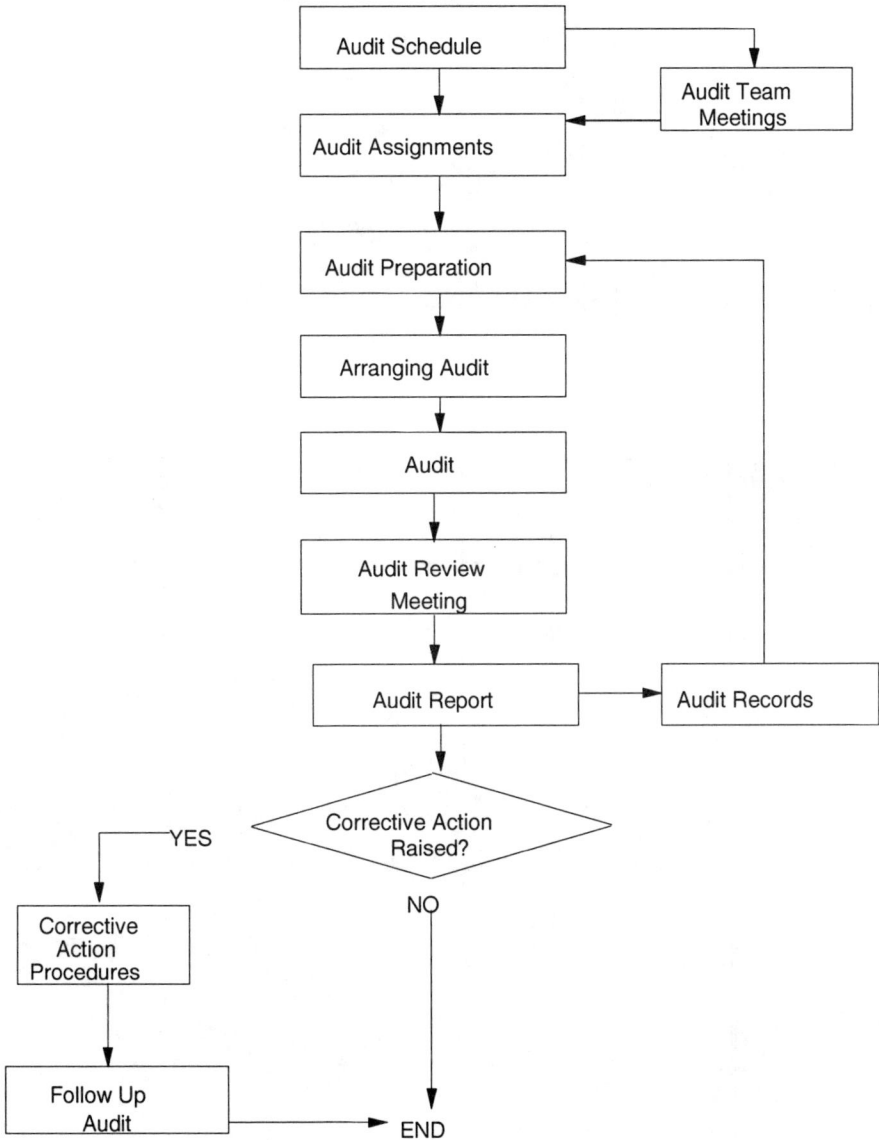

Figure 7.2 The audit process

QUALITY SYSTEM	MAIN SITE							SECOND SITE			
	QM/Admin	Sales	Design	Purchasing	Machining	Finishing	Dispatch	Purchasing	Machining A	Machining B	Assembly
Quality Manual	December										
Procedures											
QP1		January									
QP2			February September								
QP3				October				March			
QP4					April					June	August
QP5						November			May		August
QP6							July				
QP7	December										

Figure 7.3   Sample audit schedule

flexibility by having blank audit slots. However, a completely flexible schedule is no schedule at all – some structure and planning is needed.

Auditing has a particularly vital role when a quality system is first implemented and the process should be started as soon as possible (within a month of start-up) and be more frequent than after the system is bedded in. It may also be slower because of auditors' inexperience. Where the period between implementation and first assessment is less than a year, a special, contracted schedule is required so that the whole system and all areas are covered before assessment. Only in this way can there be any confidence that the system is working and ready for assessment.

Audit Team Meetings

These meetings are different from any held at the start or end of specific audits and their purpose is to consider the audit process as a whole and whether the schedule is being followed, and to discuss problems found in carrying out the work. The need for further auditor training should also be considered. In a sense the meeting is a training session and if some auditors have been on outside training courses, what they have learnt can be shared with other members of the team. Typically, such meetings are round-a-table affairs, chaired by the quality manager, and although they do not need to be over-formal, basic minutes should be kept. Quarterly meetings or even once or twice a year may be sufficient, although in the start-up period they need to be more frequent.

Audit Assignment

The quality manager needs to decide who is to carry out each audit, although in a small company there may be no choice to make (the one or two auditors are involved in every audit). A date may also need to be set for both the audit and report-back although this may have been detailed in the schedule. The scope of the audit should then be discussed with the team (the parts of the system and areas to be covered) although, unless it is unscheduled, the published plan will largely define this. Records should be kept of the assignment – the auditors concerned, the scope, date started and the date the report is received – and this is best done on a log with each audit sequentially numbered.

Audit Preparation

The auditors concerned should plan the individual audit – they should not just turn up in the area with the procedure manual in hand and decide then and there what to do. Part of this preparation should be to look at any corrective actions related to the area and changes made in the procedures concerned. The purpose of this is to identify areas where problems have been found or improvements sought and which perhaps need special attention (this is distinct from the formal follow-up audit activity to be discussed shortly). Working with a set of the relevant procedures, a checklist is then drawn up of the specifics to be covered in the audit. This is best achieved in the form of questions based on the procedures, with notes indicating any records which should be examined to check that the procedure is being followed.

In the checklist example below, the italic text is the procedure (this would not normally be written out on the checklist, although the reference number should be noted). The unbracketed text is the questions to be asked, while the bracketed text refers to things to be seen rather than asked.

Sample audit checklist

7.3.4 Listing
A list is prepared of verbatim responses from 100 questionnaires or 10% of the total number – whichever is greatest.
Can you show me an example of a listing?
How did you decide how many responses to list?
    (Listing in the job file?)

7.3.5 Code Frames
A code frame is then developed from the listing using Form 7.3.5/1
Can I now see the master copy of the code frame developed from this list?
    (Use of Form 7.3.5/1)
    (Frame in the job file?)

7.3.6 Code Frame Checking
The project manager shall check each code frame and sign to this
effect.

> (Is the code frame signed?)
> (Who has signed it? Is it the project manager?)

The checklist should be set out with space left to record what is actually found. Where the set of procedures applying to the area is extensive, it may be necessary to take a sample of them selected on a judgemental basis – eg taking into account what was found in the last audit, focusing on procedures which have recently been revised or just selecting those which seem potentially difficult to follow.

Arranging the Audit

There is obviously no point in turning up in a department to carry out an audit if all the staff are out for the day or tied up on a special task. Audits should, therefore, be arranged in advance and an appointment made (which the auditor should keep). How far in advance this should be done will vary between organisations and departments. Staff in a department may have a good reason for delaying an audit and every effort should be made to minimise disruption of normal work. However, beyond some point, legitimate postponement turns into procrastination, possibly moti-vated by concern about what may be found in the audit (such a concern, though, may indicate problems with how audit work is done) and the auditor will need to be more insistent. Beyond some point, the quality manager may have to step in to make sure the audit takes place.

Carrying Out the Audit

In principle, the actual audit consists of comparing in detail what is required in the procedures or other parts of the quality system (as noted in the checklist) with what happens in practice and recording what is found. Where there is a difference – a nonconformity – the notes should identify the details and where this was found (eg by job number). How-ever, there is rather more to this task than this bald description suggests and the techniques used by the auditor, especially in relation to dealing with the staff audited, will determine how well the work is done. Much of the skill of auditing is people handling.

The first task is to present the audit process positively. The staff being audited should understand that the purpose is to check the working of the quality system – it is not to check up on them. It should be explained that if problems are found it may well reflect that the procedures are defective or that too little attention has been given to how to implement them effectively. It can also be pointed out that it is better to find the problems internally and solve them than leave them outstanding for the assessor to pick up. This all needs saying, but it is also a matter of tone. Whatever he or she says, the message will not be believed if the auditor comes across as an interrogator. Terse conversation, abrupt questioning, an apparent objective of 'catching out' are all examples of how not to approach auditing. Such an approach may seem efficient in order to get to the root of things but it is actually counter-productive. With a 'police' approach, staff will seek to cover up problems rather than solve them – the antithesis of a quality approach.

The audit checklist defines the framework of the audit as a series of questions. However, the purpose of this is to provide a structure and asking direct, closed questions should be the exception rather than the rule. Instead, auditees should be encouraged to describe, in their own words, the steps followed in the process. Instead of asking, for example, 'can you show me the coding sheet forms?' it is better to ask 'what happens next?' at the relevant stage in the process. Auditees, however, should not be expected to be able to quote the procedures verbatim – auditing is not a memory test – and during the discussion, a copy of the relevant procedures may be to hand. Incidently, checking on the availability of the procedures and possibly checking that they are correct and up to date (probably on a sample basis) can, usefully, be part of every audit.

In an audit, the objective is to establish, through firm evidence, that the quality system is working effectively (this positive approach should be the emphasis). This evidence can take three basic forms: what auditees say they do, records chosen by auditees to demonstrate that they do what they say, and records selected by the auditors. All three forms of evidence should be sought in an audit, although not necessarily for each procedure.

Careful listening is required to establish what is said to be done and to be able to compare it with what ought to be done as per the procedures.

Just because the auditee does not use the words of the procedure does not mean he or she does not understand what is required and the auditor must carefully 'translate' the description into the sense of the procedure. However, evidence of this sort is important, since if staff plainly have no idea (or an erroneous idea) of what is supposed to be done, that part of the quality system will not be working effectively.

As discussed in the last chapter an effective procedure should involve objective evidence, after the event, that it has been followed – the various records, in the widest sense, produced by operating the system. The form of these records should be specified in the procedure and the second form of evidence is for auditees to select examples of these records so that the auditor can compare them with what is required. Obviously, auditees may well choose records that they know to be up to date and complete and this evidence should be supplemented with records selected randomly by the auditor. Since records ought to be filed methodically this ought to be practical, with the auditee's help. The auditor can also follow a job or batch through the system and establish whether, in this case, the procedures were followed and the records kept. This can even be done between departments and this may be very useful in establishing that communication and the flow of instructions are effective throughout the organisation.

From one or other sort of evidence, the audit may identify that a procedure is not working as intended; for whatever reason, staff are not doing what the system specifies. This is referred to as a 'nonconformity'. The existence or otherwise of such a nonconformity should be clear cut; either the procedure is being followed in every instance or it is not, and the auditor and auditee ought to be able to agree that this is the case. Obviously the degree of nonconformity can vary, ranging from one example of a record not completed satisfactorily (but where others are complete), through an obvious failure of one procedure to a breakdown of a whole section of the quality system. In their own work, assessors refer to the former cases as 'minor' nonconformities and the latter as 'major'. However, whatever the degree of the problem, the auditor's job is to record that it exists and not to suggest a solution or, still less, apportion blame. The records are conveniently made on the checklist together with some details of the records consulted (eg by job number). In this way, any specific instances of nonconformities can be subsequently investigated, by a separate process, if this is appropriate.

Audit Review Meeting

On completion of the audit, the outcome should be discussed with the staff audited. If the work has been done well and since the outcome should concern objective findings only, there should be no disagreement between the auditor and the auditees. If, for example, it had been found that 'code frames' (see above) had not been signed by the project manager this should not be in dispute – the signature was either there or not. The manager of this department may consider that there is good reason why this has not been done, but it is not the auditor's role to judge whether this reason for non-compliance is adequate. The audit meeting should, therefore, not be an occasion for dispute or tension. Any comments of the staff audited made at this meeting should be noted and if at this stage the formal report is prepared (as per the audit procedures), the auditee may be asked to sign this document.

On conclusion of the audit review meeting, the auditors concerned may then be responsible for preparing the formal audit report and, if required, raising corrective actions (see below). However, it is common for audit procedures to actively involve the quality manager at this stage. In this case, the auditors will informally discuss their findings with the quality manager before deciding the contents of the audit report. More specifically, the issue of corrective actions may be at the discretion of the quality manager after he or she considers the auditors' results.

The Audit Report

The notes taken during the audit provide a record of what was found in the audit and the formal audit report can be quite short – no more than a page. Conventionally audit reports are under three headings: findings, recommendations and observations.

Findings are nonconformities – where the system is not working or not being followed – and the next step in this case is to raise a corrective action. The details of the non-compliance can be recorded on the audit report or it may be sufficient just to refer to a numbered corrective action form which includes a description of the problem.

Corrective actions are the subject of a separate chapter (see Chapter 11) and the detail is not discussed here. One important point, however, is that a nonconformity does not necessarily mean that the system – a procedure – is faulty and needs changing. At least as likely is a problem of implementation – the staff are just not following what should be a reasonable procedure. There are various reasons why this might be so, but the most common is simply a lack of knowledge – they do not know what is supposed to be done – and the remedy is further training. This need not be elaborate; often pointing out the problem, even in the course of the audit, solves it. Strictly speaking the auditor or quality manager should not pre-judge the cause of the problem. It may be that the cause appears to be that someone is just not following a perfectly reasonable procedure, but on further investigation it is possible that there is good reason for this and that the procedure is not effective; the corrective action investigation should uncover the true position. However, the quality manager can often use some discretion in this respect. Where it seems very reasonable that the problem lies with an individual rather than the system, it may be effective to have that person investigate the problem; they are then aware that they should be following the procedure and if there is a problem in doing this, it gives them an opportunity to say so. However, this approach should not be taken too far; auditing or corrective action should not be used as a disciplinary device with faults 'punished' by aptly named corrective actions.

Recommendations in the audit report are smaller findings, perhaps very minor nonconformities that are not considered to be sufficiently serious to justify raising a corrective action. In the example used for the checklist, perhaps it was found that a signature had been missed from one coding frame but that all the others were correct. The line between findings and recommendations is obviously arbitrary and requires judgement by the auditors and quality manager, although, over time, some consistency should evolve. Recommendations, in this sense, are also not proposals for solving problems – as discussed earlier this is not the auditor's role. Rather than finding solutions, audit recommendations can be seen as a means of identifying potential problems before they really happen.

Finally, observations, the third sort of entry on an audit report, identify subjects which ought to be considered – nothing was specifically wrong but possibly there is potential for an improvement in working methods. This may be apparent to the auditor or even suggested by the staff working in the area covered in the audit. An observation may also be a pointer to the focus in future audits. Again, however, the auditor should not become involved in problem-solving; having made an observation it is for others to take action (if any is needed).

A copy of the completed audit report should be given to and discussed with the manager of the area covered in the audit and this may be linked into the procedure for investigating any corrective actions raised as a result of the audit. The quality manager will also receive a copy of the report and file it, possibly together with the detailed notes made by the auditors (alternatively the auditors may be responsible for keeping these). The report will then be available when planning the next audit in that particular area.

Follow-up Audits

While auditing itself is not meant to solve problems, it is part of a system of finding solutions. If nonconformities are found, the corrective action procedure is used to investigate the problem and recommend an effective solution. Auditing, however, has a further role and that is to establish whether a solution *has* been successfully implemented – has the corrective action been successful? This could be established in the next scheduled audit of the particular area. However, this may well be in a year's time and this is too long to wait to discover whether an effective solution has been found – if it has not, a possibly serious problem will still be present. There is a need, therefore, to have a special follow-up audit procedure.

Follow-up audits should be carried out within a particular period of issuing a corrective action – eg 40 days – and this should be specified in the audit procedures. Unlike full audits, follow-ups have a narrow focus and are just concerned with the nonconformities identified in the original audit and establishing whether the system is now being followed. If the corrective action led to a change in the procedures, the follow-up will therefore be concerned with whether this change is effective, while if better implementation of a procedure was the proposed solution, this too will be checked out. If the follow-up audit indicates that the corrective action has been successful and the system is working effectively, the audit is then regarded as 'closed off'.

A follow-up audit may, however, find that the corrective action has not been successful. Sometimes this is because there has not been enough time to solve the problem – this may particularly be the case where a change in procedures is required. More seriously, however, the revised procedure may be found not to be effective or attempts to improve the implementation of an effective procedure may not have succeeded. The logic in any of these situations is for a further corrective action to be raised and the process to be repeated, and if necessary repeated again (and again) until the problem is solved. However, it is in practice not satisfactory to build up a whole file of incomplete corrective actions which never appear to be solved – if this happens the quality system is not working at a fundamental level and the quality manager must ensure that something effective is done. This may involve referring the matter to a management review meeting (see Chapter 13) and involving other senior managers in the solution.

As with a full audit, a follow-up should involve preparing a brief report, in this case focused on the outcome of the corrective action (eg whether it is 'complete' or not), and the quality manager should file this with other audit records. The manager of the department concerned should of course, be formally told of the outcome.

8

MONITORING OPERATIONAL NONCONFORMITIES

In the previous chapter we discussed how nonconformities are identified through auditing. However, these are only one type of nonconformity – *system nonconformities,* where the quality system is not working effectively. There are also three other sorts of nonconformity which need controlling through a quality system. In this chapter we are concerned with *operational nonconformities*; things which go wrong in carrying out the business and processes of the organisation – faulty products are one obvious example. The remaining two types of nonconformity are discussed in the next two chapters and are those which relate to supplier problems (Chapter 9) and customer complaints (Chapter 10). Arguably, the latter is not really a separate category but one way in which operational problems or problems originating with suppliers become manifest. However, customer complaints clearly have to be taken very seriously and, for this reason, are considered in a separate chapter.

MAJOR AND MINOR OPERATIONAL NONCONFORMITIES

Some problems are so big that they cannot be ignored; they hit you hard and you have to react in some way. Within organisations, these are the major operational nonconformities. Examples include serious failures of the plant, projects running far behind timetable or their budgets being grossly overshot, and serious faults in products or services delivered to customers or otherwise requiring major remedial work. When these sorts of problems happen, there is no question of ignoring them; managers and staff have to do something at least to deal with the immediate crisis and salvage whatever can be got out of the disaster. Hopefully, these sorts of operational nonconformity will be the exception rather than the rule and although analysis of the problems (through corrective actions) may identify organisational causes which made them inevitable, there is an element of randomness about them or at least about when they occur. There is, however, another sort of operational nonconformity. These happen all the time, probably have little impact in isolation and may be largely unnoticed or their solution neglected. These are minor operational nonconformities.

Examples of minor operational nonconformities are found in all organisations and may be present to some degree all the time. In manufacturing, this sort of nonconformity often takes the form of small variations in the output of a process with some products outside defined tolerance levels. These may be detected at inspection stages and rejected or corrected there and then, or they may pass through, undetected, into the final product but without any sort of catastrophic impact. In service businesses there are comparable examples such as the number of drafts of a document which have to be prepared before it is accepted, minor over-runs of timetable and budgets in parts or all of the process and disruptions caused by the need to clarify inadequate instructions between departments.

A characteristic of minor operational nonconformities is that taken one by one and in isolation they have little impact – had the single nonconformity not occurred, the efficiency of the whole process or the quality of the final product might have been better, but only to an insignificant degree. Of course, sometimes a minor fault or variation can have unforeseen and dramatic consequences – for the want of a nail a kingdom was lost, or so folklore had it about King Richard's defeat by Henry Tudor – and in complex operating systems such chaos theory effects may need to be a concern. However, these sorts of nonconformities are not really minor because they develop into something big and disastrous and cannot be ignored. More commonly, however, the effect of minor nonconformities in the operation are cumulative and although the impact of each in isolation is negligible, they can build up and in aggregation produce significant negative effects.

The two main cumulative effects of minor operational nonconformities are on the quality of the final output and on efficiency. As minor nonconformities aggregate, the average quality of the final output will decline and customers will become less satisfied. The nature of these problems may be such that customer complaints are not triggered – the minor setting problem was sorted out by the customer and although irritated he is not so annoyed as to go to the trouble of contacting the supplier. However, if not identified and dealt with, these problems will tend to be ongoing with the effect that customer perception of the company will tend to go down rather than up and the organisation's standing in its market will gradually decline relative to competitors. This will eventually translate into declining market shares and, therefore, have a very real cost.

Minor operational nonconformities tend also to reduce internal efficiency as well as any effect they may have on final output quality. This may take the form of a slowly rising (or, for that matter, not a falling) scrap level and this involves increasing costs of wasted materials and wasted resources and operating time. Alternatively, in businesses where visible scrap piles are not a feature of the process (eg many service businesses), the cumulative effect is an increase in reworking – doing jobs twice because the first attempt was not right. Again this leads to an increase of costs through, literally, wasted time.

Taken together, these sorts of effects from minor operational nonconformities will eventually be noticed (eg through the declining financial performance of the organisation), and by this time their costs may be substantial. However, the causes of the problem may by now not be clear; it can be very difficult to check back to identify the succession of minor nonconformities which were to blame. A better approach, therefore, is to incorporate into the system – the quality system – some method of monitoring minor nonconformities and doing something about them before they build up into significant and wasteful costs. This approach is effectively a formal requirement of ISO 9000 and any organisation adopting the Standard will need to build in some attempt at the monitoring of nonconformities. However, like some other aspects of the Standard, meeting this requirement can be more a matter of form than substance – doing it to gain the certificate rather than for any real benefit. Often, what determines whether any real benefit is obtained is the organisation's general culture in respect to problem-solving.

TWO PROBLEM-SOLVING CULTURES

Broadly there are two approaches to problem-solving – firefighting and continuous improvement. In any organisation both are likely to be present to some degree but an outsider, aware of these cultures, will usually be able to decide quickly which predominates.

Firefighting is concerned with solving the problem, whatever it is, as quickly as possible and being in a state of readiness to deal with the next outbreak, wherever it happens. The problems are, therefore, expected but not anticipated. Indeed the view within this culture is that problems occur owing to factors beyond practical control; it is accepted that something will always go wrong and nothing much can be done about it in advance. Often, it is thought that problems are, at bottom, due to human error and deficient human nature. The tone is, therefore, one of fatalism about the occurrence of problems but coupled with strongly reactive responses – once they do happen the firefighting team is brought into action. However, because little is done in a firefighting culture to anticipate problems or to seek long-term solutions, the whole thing becomes self-fulfilling. Because the effort and resources go into firefighting rather than prevention, fires inevitably break out.

A firefighting culture is a heroic one. The corporate heroes are the firemen, the managers ready to roll up their sleeves and get involved, to take on responsibility for solving the crisis, to keep at it until it is right again and get it done even if it kills them (literally or figuratively). In strong firefighting cultures, it is the firemen who build reputations and get promoted and the top management are likely to be mainly in this mould. Given this outlook, elevation of the firemen is also essential – because little or nothing is done beyond putting out the fires, the firemen's skills will be called for over and over again.

Firemen and firefighting cultures may pay lip-service to the need to prevent fires as well as put them out, with perhaps talk about long-term problem-solving as an ideal. But little or no emphasis will be put into these areas in practice. Partly this is because the belief in real improvement is too weak but it also reflects that there is little kudos in working in this way – it is the firemen who are the heros and who are rewarded. Pressed for a reason for not taking a longer-term view, lack of time is often given as the excuse but this is part of a vicious circle – because all the time is taken up with firefighting there is no time for other things. The question might be asked, how is it that time can always be found to put things right or do them again, but there is never time to find ways of doing them right in the first place?

The basic approach is different in a culture of long-term improvement. Here operational nonconformities are not seen just as problems to solve here and now but evidence that there is a deficiency in the working methods and quality system. There is an implicit assumption that such deficiencies can be solved and solved for good and that once the root causes are tackled, problems – or at least the specific problems – will go, with overall quality and efficiency improved. Nonconformities are, there-fore, almost welcomed as indicators of a need for positive change.

The emphasis in a continuous improvement culture is on recording, investigation, analysis and thought-out solutions. Status and rewards now go to those with these skills. Nor does this approach imply a static environment – speedy reactions to changes in technology and market demand can be built into the approach. However, there is some danger, in this culture, of managers becoming isolated from the real world and tending to see the production of elegant solutions as an end in itself. They work towards these even while the house is burning down around them.

As we mentioned, either the firefighting or continuous improvement culture will tend to predominate. However, no organisation can avoid having some element of each. Fires do have to be put out, usually before a long-term solution can be found or even considered. If a customer complains, some means of making him or her happy or at least less unhappy is the first priority before considering how future recurrence can be prevented. If a processing stage is defective, reworking perhaps to an 'impossible' timetable may be essential as a first step. Even in an organ-isation committed to continuous and long-term improvement, the fireman, therefore, has a place and his (or her) value needs to be recognised. Similarly, in a firefighting culture, long-term solutions cannot be ignored for ever. If nothing else, some patterns in problems will become obvious and long-term lessons learnt even by the most reactive of managers.

In many organisations, it is the firefighting skills which are in place and it is more likely that the need is to strengthen the continuous improve-ment approach. One of the quality manager's roles is to do just this, through direct action or by encouraging others. In either case, the starting point for long-term improvement is keeping adequate records – the evidence needed to identify the problems and find solutions.

QUALITY RECORDS AND OPERATIONAL NONCONFORMITIES

ISO 9000 requires quality records to be kept as part of operating a quality system. This is set out under various headings in the Standard including *4.9 Process control.* In some organisations, however, quality records are kept because it is a requirement of the Standard and for little other reason – the records are not used constructively. It is in such organisations that ISO 9000 is most likely to be criticised as bureaucratic, to involve endless form-filling for form-filling's sake. It is not surprising, though, that with no intention to get anything out of the records, no intrinsic benefit is obtained. This is a pity because quality records provide the data for identifying problems and setting priorities for analysing them and, in the long term, help to produce lasting solutions and improvement.

Quality records, at least in the operating process area, show significant readings taken while the product or service was being produced – measurements of the output or the process leading to it, the results of inspections, the time taken to complete stages in the process, the level of input required including labour, etc. All this demonstrates that the correct procedures have been followed in assuring the quality of the output. Another way of looking at this data, however, is that it is a record of operational nonconformities: products or batches with measurements outside tolerance limits, faults identified in inspection and the resulting scrap or reworking levels, longer than standard or average process times and input levels above those which were anticipated. Quality records, therefore, identify where problems or nonconformities have occurred as well as showing what steps have been taken to do things right.

The system can build in continuous monitoring of these process records and require some action to be instigated wherever and whenever nonconformities are found. Such an approach may be appropriate in some small businesses or where the nature of what is being produced is in small unit throughput. However, in most organisations the number of nonconformities identified through the records is likely to be substantial and it will be impossible to take action in each and every case. Nor would such action pay off even if it could be taken – some nonconformities may be very unusual or random and without any underlying systematic cause which can be addressed. Generally, therefore, it is necessary to prioritise the identified nonconformities and concentrate action where solutions are likely to have the greatest pay-off.

Nonconformities can be prioritised in various ways, including simply picking out those which appear self-evidently important. Major noncon-formities, the real disasters, obviously come into this category and need immediate corrective action, both for short-term salvaging and long-term prevention. Where, however, the record system identifies significant numbers of minor nonconformities which can be categorised into classes, types or groups and where each problem is roughly of equal value or cost, a Pareto curve approach is a useful tool for setting priorities. This is illustrated in Figure 8.1.

The figure could represent almost any operation – eg the results of a vehicle dealership's pre-delivery inspections – and shows as vertical bars the number of times each type of fault (eg paintwork, trim, electrics, etc) was found, in descending order. The line shows the cumulative level of faults and is the 'Pareto curve'. As in most such systems (not just nonconformity analysis) the cumulative curve demonstrates something approaching an '80/20' rule – 20 per cent of the types of faults (faults 1, 2, 3 and 4) account for 80 per cent of all faults and, conversely, many (faults 5 to 20) account for only a few per cent. With this sort of analysis, it is fairly obvious where attention in an improvement exercise should be focused, at least initially. In Figure 8.1, if we can stop faults 1 and 2 occurring or significantly reduce their occurrence we will make a major impact on the reject or reworking levels.* However, the improvement process need not stop there. Once we found why faults 1 and 2 occur and have removed the causes, we can draw up a new chart and Pareto curve and focus on what are now the major problem areas – the new '20 per cent'.

---

* We must emphasise again, however, that this type of analysis assumes that all problems or faults are of equal worth or cost. In the example, it would be a different matter if fault 8 related to steering and not solving the problem could lead, potentially, to a fatal accident.

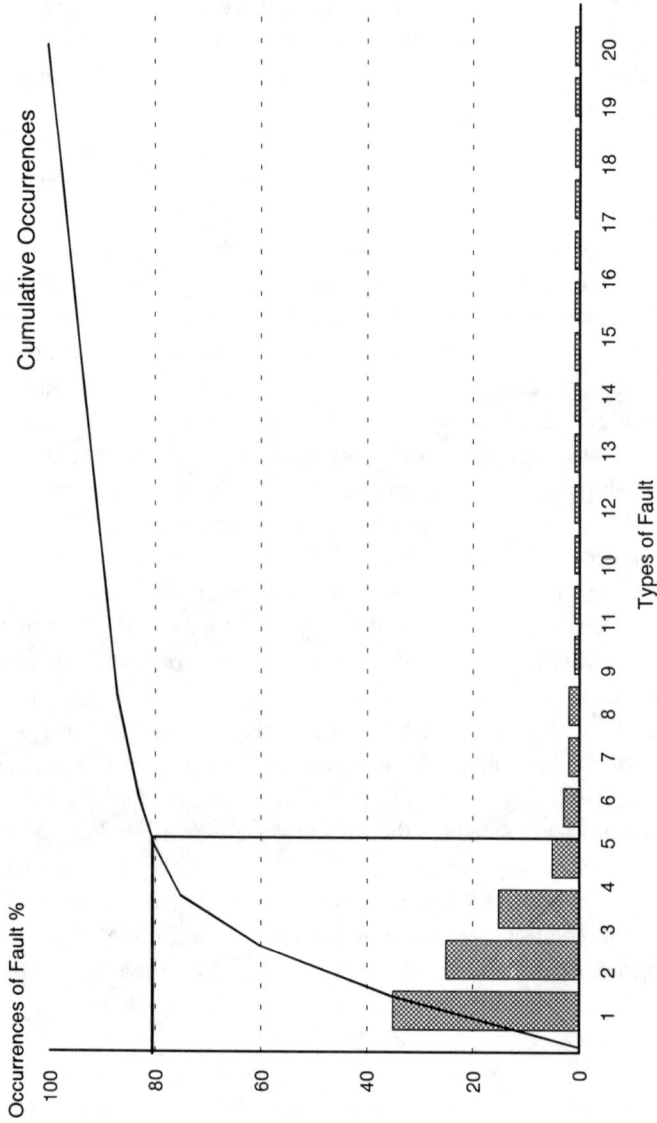

Figure 8.1 Example of Pareto curve analysis

To make effective use of quality/nonconformity records, therefore, some system of setting priorities is needed when deciding which should be selected for further or initial investigation. One effective tool is Pareto curve analysis. However, there is another question of priorities which comes before this – which records should be taken and kept in the first place?

WHAT SHOULD BE RECORDED?

While ISO 9000 requires records to be kept as part of the operating procedures (ie process control), there is no indication in the Standard of which specific readings should be taken. Nor can there be in a standard meant to apply to any type of organisation or business; what is important to record in a marketing consultancy will be quite different from what is needed in a steel forging process. Deciding what specifically is to be recorded calls for judgement and an understanding of the particular operation. This is why complaints that ISO 9000 requires 'too many' records to be kept so much miss the point. ISO 9000 does not require *any* specific process records to be kept and if those which are kept are 'no use' whose fault is that? The organisation concerned has chosen to keep 'useless' records. Either they are intrinsically useless or rendered so because nothing useful is done with them.

In any quality system, the records needed and how they are to be kept should be set out in the procedures. When the system is first designed, careful analysis should be carried out to identify what *provisionally* should be recorded and once the system is implemented it is these records which provide the evidence of operational nonconformities which can be analysed, investigated and for which, in due course, lasting remedies can be found. However, the record system should not be thought of as fixed for all time and should be regularly reviewed and modified where this seems appropriate. There are two main strands to this: reducing the record-keeping in areas where nothing useful seems to come out of the work, and adding additional types of records to cover unanticipated nonconformities.

When the operation of a procedure is reviewed, it may be found that some of the records show no or very few instances of nonconformities; the output is always to specification or very nearly so. In this case, therefore, it is legitimate to question the value of taking the record. Why do the work involved in taking the reading? Even if the record is produced automatically (eg as part of a computer-controlled operation) someone will have to at least spend time examining it (if they do not it is certainly useless). Instances of such unproductive records may be raised by the managers and staff involved, by the internal audit team, by corrective action investigations or through a special review undertaken by the quality manager or the management team. However they are found, the value of retaining them should be critically considered and often the procedure changed to remove them from the system.

The opposite case is where, after a quality system is implemented, it becomes apparent that problems are occurring in unanticipated areas and where the need for quality records had not been envisaged. This shortfall may become apparent through the investigation of linked problems, customer complaints, the results of audits, special reviews of procedures or just by a member of staff recognising the gap. Again, the system should be changed; in this case to include a type of record if this seems appropriate and potentially useful. The same may apply when an entirely new procedure is introduced; this may call for an additional form of monitoring and record-keeping. However – and this point also applies to the initial design of the system – record-keeping has a cost and a practical limit. You cannot, physically or economically, record everything and, in the end, a judgement has to be made that keeping the record has potential benefits (ie through reducing operating nonconformities) which outweigh the cost. Once made and implemented, the decision to add a record should be in turn reviewed alongside those data requirements already part of the system. In other words, what records should be kept should always be questioned and, if appropriate, changed. In this respect no part of the system should be sacrosanct.

RESPONSIBILITIES AND FINDING SOLUTIONS

Like the auditing system, monitoring operational nonconformities should identify problems. Solving them should be kept formally separate. The process of investigating and finding solutions to nonconformities, which monitoring identifies as significant, is through a corrective action procedure and this is discussed in Chapter 11. However, if this point is to be reached at all, the records and data must be monitored and the decision taken that an operational nonconformity justifies cranking up the corrective action procedure. This will not happen unless these responsibilities are firmly assigned and possibly embedded in the system.

The quality manager clearly has a particular responsibility for ensuring that the nonconformities are monitored – it is part of being responsible for the efficient administration of the whole system. In some cases, this responsibility may be best discharged by the quality manager or one of his or her own staff. This may be the best approach in some organisations and in some areas of organisations – at least, this way, the work is likely to be done effectively. However, the downside of this is to strengthen the false notion that quality matters are the responsibility of the quality manager and no one else. This should not be so and it may be worth shifting some of the work of monitoring to line management for no other reason than to make sure that the quality system is widely 'owned'. Moreover, nonconformities are first and foremost the responsibility of managers and staff working in the areas where they arise. How can a manager be doing the job well if he or she has no idea of what is going wrong?

Whether the responsibility for monitoring operational nonconformities is the quality manager's or line managers' the audit process should cover whether this is done effectively (and, therefore, if necessary, initiate the process of ensuring it is going to be done effectively in future – including changing the system if this is needed). Where the responsibilities for nonconformity monitoring are explicitly defined in the system, auditing them would in any case be routine where the procedures or area covered are within the scope of the audit. Where responsibilities for monitoring are not fully specified (and it is not always convenient or practical to do so), checking out what happens in practice should be specifically included in some audit assignments.

PURCHASING AND SUPPLIER MONITORING

9

The previous chapter discussed nonconformities which arise internally within the operating process. This chapter discusses another sort of nonconformity – those which come into an organisation as part of the goods and services purchased from outside suppliers. We also consider the broader requirement to include purchasing as a whole in a quality system and the quality manager's role in this area.

THE IMPORTANCE OF PURCHASING AND ISO 9000 REQUIREMENTS

In many businesses, purchased goods and services rather than internal processes represent most of the value of the final output, and even where this is not the case, the quality of the final product is very dependent on what comes into the process from outside. Controlling outside supplies, whether these are goods or services, is, therefore, a critical requirement and needs to be part of any effective quality system. Arguably, this aspect of quality assurance is also more difficult than managing internal processes. In principle, the latter can be tightly controlled just because they are internal, while the quality of incoming goods and services is in the hands of independent and often remote organisations.

The need to control purchasing and suppliers is also a requirement of

ISO 9000 – mainly set out under heading *4.6 Purchasing*. Specifically, the requirements cover the three subheadings discussed below.

Selection and Evaluation (heading *4.6.2*)

Suppliers* must be selected on the basis of their ability to meet quality requirements. When an organisation first sets up a quality system it is reasonable to use as a criterion for the selection of adequate suppliers their past performance. If a company has been a satisfactory supplier for years, this is as good a reason as any to 'select' it for inclusion in an approved supplier list. New suppliers, however, will require more positive evaluation before their selection and this may include a review or audit of their own quality assurance systems (there is no requirement for an ISO 9000 registered organisation to use a ISO 9000 supplier but registration might be regarded as a positive indicator), technical evaluations and product trials. Once suppliers have been selected, there should be mechanisms to ensure that purchasing is restricted to approved suppliers – approved supplier lists, perhaps supplemented with a special procedure for authorising purchases from non-listed sources, is a common approach.

Supplier evaluation also needs to be ongoing. There is clearly no point going to all the trouble of an initial approval system if the performance of suppliers is then just ignored. Some means is needed to ensure that suppliers' ability to meet quality requirements is reviewed continuously or at least periodically and appropriate action taken on the basis of this evaluation (this is implied rather than explicitly stated in the relevant part of ISO 9000).

Purchasing Records (heading *4.6.3*)

Quality of supply implies the ability of the supplier to meet an organisation's requirements. Clearly this cannot be evaluated unless the requirement is defined and ISO 9000 requires records to be kept of what is

---

* Suppliers generally are referred to in ISO 9000 as 'subcontractors' – this term has no special meaning – the 'supplier' is the organisation implementing the quality system.

ordered. Apart from any quality concerns, knowing precisely what is ordered is also good commercial practice – you cannot complain that the delivery does not match the order if there is no or an inadequate record of what this was. This requirement does not have to mean that every order is placed in writing, and in some circumstances and in some types of business this might be inconvenient or contrary to well established business practice. However, where a written order is not given to the supplier, the details need recording in some other way and most businesses will find a firmly controlled system of written orders effective on both quality and commercial grounds. Often the major effect of introducing a formal quality system into purchasing is not to change the policy of placing written orders but to ensure that it is followed in every case.

The purchasing heading (*4.6*) of ISO 9000 does not specify that records are to be kept of deliveries or the degree to which these match orders and requirements. However, the need for these records is defined under another heading of the Standard (*4.10*) and we shall discuss this shortly.

Verification of Purchased Product (heading *4.6.4*)

The requirements for verification of purchased product as set out under the purchasing heading refer to rather specialised circumstances rather than arrangements which are generally common. These circumstances are where it is agreed with the supplier that the goods or the process of making them will be inspected by the buyer at the supplier's premises, or where it is agreed with both the supplier and the final customer (ie your customer) that the customer will inspect the supplier's premises. Often neither of these arrangements apply or are appropriate. However, under a separate heading of the Standard – *4.10.2 Receiving inspection and testing* – there is a requirement to inspect purchased goods and services as they are supplied and delivered, and this activity involves keeping records to show the results of such inspections or tests. The type of inspection or testing will vary with the type of goods or service and perhaps the degree of quality assurance exercised by the supplier (ie confidence in the supplier to supply consistently to specification), but as a minimum the required record system should show that the delivery is satisfactory – meets the specified requirements – or not. These records then provide data for monitoring supplier performance.

The ISO 9000 requirements for purchasing need to be implemented through effective procedures and in most systems there will be a distinct section of the procedure manual covering purchasing and often this will include or refer to an approved supplier list. Purchasing procedures should be audited in the same way as other parts of a quality system and the scope of these audits should include whether any suppliers used* have been approved (ie are on the approved list or otherwise), whether there are adequate records of each order placed and whether deliveries have been inspected in the ways specified in the procedures. Any problems found in these areas through the audits should be dealt with in the same way as any other system nonconformities (see Chapters 7 and 11).

The routine work of evaluating new suppliers, placing orders and inspecting deliveries will not normally involve the quality manager on a day-to-day basis and will be carried out, instead, by the purchasing department (if there is one) or other line staff. However, the quality manager has a responsibility to ensure the quality system and procedures work effectively. Apart from ensuring that effective audits are carried out, this can involve tasks such as compiling and periodically reviewing the approved supplier list (the purchasing procedures are likely to include an annual review and revision of the list), reviewing how major suppliers are evaluated and perhaps arranging and taking part in audit visits to these organisations. In addition, however, the quality manager has a responsibility to ensure supplier performance is effectively monitored and that action is taken on the basis of this work. In doing this, the quality manager will be moving beyond at least the explicit requirements of ISO 9000 (arguably, the Standard here is stronger on requiring records to be kept than in ensuring effective action is taken on the basis of the evidence collected) but, often, for only a marginal increase in effort, the quality system will lead to real benefits rather than just produce records to meet the demands of ISO 9000. In other words, the quality manager will be acting as a champion of quality rather than just as a system guardian.

---

* Strictly speaking, the quality system only needs to cover supplies with some direct relevance to the quality of the final product; other goods and services (eg housekeeping items) can be kept outside the scope of the quality system procedures. In practice, however, most organisations will find it more convenient and effective to include all supplies in the system.

MONITORING METHODS

The objective of monitoring, in relation to suppliers, is to identify relevant nonconformities and wherever possible to take action to reduce the future occurrence of these problems as well as to put right any identified deficiencies. Monitoring of suppliers, like other forms of monitoring, therefore, has a long-term emphasis as well as seeking necessary and immediate remedies. We favour using a scoring system as an effective system of monitoring, but before discussing this approach others will be more briefly mentioned. It should also be noted that scoring goes beyond what is required in ISO 9000.

Probably the simplest form of monitoring is one based on complaints made to suppliers. Where the delivery fails to match the specification, the managers and staff involved are likely to complain to the supplier and will certainly do so if the mismatch is serious. To use this as a basis of monitoring, all that is necessary is that the complaint to the supplier is documented. This might take the form of a copy of a letter to the supplier or a note of any verbal complaint made. Purchasing or other line staff will be involved in obtaining an immediate remedy to the complaint – sending back the faulty goods and requesting a replacement, having the supplier carry out remedial work or possibly negotiating monetary compensation. The quality manager's role, however, will be more long term and may include initiating a corrective action to investigate how the chances of recurrence might be lessened. However, where the problem is not very severe a corrective action may not need to be initiated on the strength of just one complaint and instead the complaint records will be reviewed to identify where attention should be focused (and corrective actions raised). This might relate to individual suppliers (those with a number of complaints raised) or a particular type of purchase.

A complaint-based system of supplier monitoring can be effective but it does have defects. One is that it concerns only deficiencies and nonconformities and does not build in any concept of excellence. With this system, bad suppliers may be dealt with but there is no contribution to building relationships with good suppliers. Also, complaints are probably only raised when some threshold of dissatisfaction is passed. Suppliers and supplies may not be perfect but not so bad that the manager concerned feels it appropriate (or is willing to go to the trouble) to complain.

The receiving inspection records (required by ISO 9000) also provide a method of monitoring suppliers and their performance. What form the inspection or testing takes will depend on the nature of the supplies and what is laid down in the procedures, but will show key parameters of the goods or service and, by implication, where they do not meet specifications – ie where there are nonconformities. These records can be used in exactly the same way as the process records discussed in Chapter 8. They can be reviewed periodically and nonconformities requiring further action dealt with through the corrective action procedure. Often this will take the form of prioritising certain types or instances of nonconformities and this can involve simple inspection of the records or more elaborate Pareto analysis (see Chapter 8).

Reviewing receiving inspection records is an effective approach to monitoring suppliers and generally more thorough than a complaint-based system. Like the latter system, however, it is negative in approach and identifies deficient rather than good suppliers. Also the work of reviewing the records can be considerable and comes in peaks and troughs. Moreover, because it involves special effort, it may be not be always done as regularly and as quickly as it ought to be.

A system of supplier scoring is based on every delivery being evaluated in the form of a numerical score. At its simplest, this score might be on only one dimension – the degree to which the delivery, overall, matches the requirements. Typically, the score is awarded from a range of 1 to 10 where 1 corresponds to very poor and 10 to excellent. However, different ranges can be used instead, eg out of 5 or 100, or from -2 to +2 with 0 as a neutral position. Such one-dimensional systems are simple to use and require the minimum of work.

A limitation of just using one overall score is that it does not identify in which aspects the suppliers fall down (or for that matter excel) and this is important if effective remedial action is to be taken. A more sophisticated scoring system, therefore, gives separate scores for different aspects of conformity to requirements. Typical dimensions might include: dimensional conformity, finish, other technical aspects, packaging, timeliness (whether delivery is to schedule) and supplier follow-up (if this is relevant) – anything which seems critical in the supply. Clearly the relevant dimensions will vary depending on the product or service supplied and it may be appropriate to use different ones for different types of supply (though probably grouped under common headings).

Having scored each delivery, a composite or average score can then be calculated for each supplier or, for that matter, type of supply. Where a one-dimensional scoring system is used, it is a simple matter to keep a running average (adding the latest score and re-averaging). If a multi-dimension scoring system is in place, an overall average score can be calculated for all the dimensions. This average can be simple (ie the scores on, say, five dimensions added and divided by five) or it can be weighted. The latter takes into account that each dimension is not of equal value and, therefore, the more important (based usually on a judgement) are given a higher weighting. In a system using five dimensions the score for the dimension considered most important might be given a weight of 5 (ie the score multiplied by 5) etc, down to the least important, which is given a weight of 1 (the score multiplied by 1). The overall average would then be the sum of the products of the scores multiplied by the weights divided by the sum of the weights (in this case 15).

However the average scores are calculated, they enable comparisons to be made and put in place an effective system of supplier monitoring. The comparisons can be between suppliers and take the form of a performance league table or can be for one supplier over time with the score plotted monthly or for any convenient period. This enables any improvement or decline in supplier performance to be identified with the degree of change quantified. Comparisons can also be across types of supply as well as suppliers and this will show where problems are most likely to occur. Where a multi-dimensional scoring system is used, comparisons can be looked at in more detail to see whether there is a pattern in the type of faults. Such detailed analysis can be on an exception basis, eg carried out for suppliers at the bottom of the league or whose overall score has fallen by more than so many points within a period.

An obvious objection to a supplier scoring system is that it is all a lot of extra work. But is this in fact the case? There is a need (ie in ISO 9000) to verify all deliveries in some way and recording this in the form of numerical scores is often as convenient a way as any other. The scores can be given by the staff who would, in any case, be involved in verification and after only brief training they will probably find scoring an effective and convenient method (one purpose of training ought to be an attempt to standardise the basis of scoring, as much as possible, where several people are involved in the work). The aggregation and averaging of delivery scores may be a responsibility of the purchasing department or the quality manager and will constitute an additional task. However, with computerisation, the chore involved can be much reduced. Anyone who is reasonably adept with a standard PC database or spreadsheet package should be able to easily design an effective system. Alternatively a software house can be commissioned to design one. The computerised record system may also be extended to recording the scores given for individual deliveries/orders and with this approach a scoring system may involve less work than other systems of purchase verification.

WORKING WITH SUPPLIERS

Whether a scoring system or some other method of monitoring is in place, the work should not be an end in itself. The result should be more than impressive looking graphs decorating the quality manager's office. Instead, supplier monitoring should be used to bring about real improvements in the quality of goods and services brought into the organisation and incorporated into the final products.

One use of a monitoring system can be to remove poor suppliers from the approved list.* If a scoring system is involved, the bottom 5 or 10 per cent of suppliers in the league table might be replaced (assuming this is commercially practical – see below) or those whose performance scores fall by a set amount might also be struck off the list. These decisions might be *ad hoc* and possibly involve a joint review by the purchasing manager and quality manager, or they might be systematised and built into procedures (although some discretion is surely required). In this way, by removing the poor suppliers, the overall performance of suppliers should improve providing there is an adequate choice of alternatives to replace the deficient ones. However, this is a rather negative way of working with suppliers.

Increasingly, the emphasis in purchasing is on long-term supplier relationships based on a partnership rather than an adversarial model. Therefore, rather than using monitoring just to weed out the bad, the

---

* Suppliers might also be removed for other reasons including a catastrophic performance or commercial malpractice.

approach can be used to improve relationships and work with suppliers to overcome problems jointly and enhance quality. On pragmatic grounds alone this is often better. Buying from a new supplier always has an element of risk and uncertainty and quite possibly this alternative will prove to be no better than the 'bad', displaced supplier. Moreover, faults in supplies are quite commonly the result of mismanagement by the customer as well as the supplier – the order may have been poorly specified or intermediate work may not have been checked adequately by the buyer – and these sorts of problems will not be overcome if the only response is simply to stop dealing with the presumed culprit. Arguably, any investigation of faults in supply should start with the internal processes. Finally a system based just on punishing bad suppliers does nothing to encourage good ones; at the most all they know is that the customer often changes supplier, apparently on a whim, and perhaps, therefore, the account does not justify their fullest attention.

Positive approaches to dealing with suppliers and jointly seeking improvements are based on an openness in the relationship. In particular, the results of monitoring or other scoring should be communicated to suppliers. The league table can be published and circulated among the companies on the approved list or variations in the average scores of each supplier fed back. Communicating this data is in itself an incentive to improvement. For a start it shows the buyer is proactive and goes to some trouble to monitor performance. Also, it is reasonable to assume that nearly all suppliers want to be well rather than poorly thought of by their customers. Communicating a score or other measure of performance, therefore, is itself an incentive for the supplier to improve.

Additionally, the procedures which follow from supplier scores should be known to the suppliers. For example, it may be that if a supplier score falls by more than so much (or its league position slips) an investigation is carried out by the purchaser (ie a corrective action procedure is initiated) and possibly this will involve or lead to a factory visit, extra inspections, resubmitting samples for trial, etc. With these ground rules laid down, the supplier knows what to expect and the objectives sought from the procedure. Obviously, there is also a penalty aspect to all this and this will be a deterrent to poor performance.

The above is a form of using supplier scoring and monitoring as a stick to encourage improvement but the carrot has a place as well. Good scores are themselves an incentive to the supplier, if only as a reminder that effort is needed to keep a strong position. But the incentive can also be more tangible. This can take monetary forms such as shorter payment terms (while this has a cost, the quality benefits it brings also have a positive value) or payment by direct debit with the minimum of paperwork. Rewards can also be in other tangible forms, eg advertising features, automatic ordering procedures or reduced inspection with benefits to both sides.

Customer monitoring can, therefore, be used in various ways to improve quality. However, it should not be forgotten that the relationship between supplier and purchaser is also a commercial one. Prices and terms have to be agreed and sometimes haggled. Although the relationship may be a partnership some gamesmanship will be involved as well. The link between this and, for example, being open with the scoring must, therefore, be fully thought through; suppliers should not be given the signal that an improving score is a reason to up the price, and even with favoured suppliers, some testing of the market may still be needed from time to time (although it may be worth paying some premium for enhanced quality since the benefits may reduce costs elsewhere). Commercial reality also intrudes in other ways, including in the recognition that the choice of potential suppliers is not infinite. In an extreme case there is a limit to what can be done about a poor supplier if, effectively, there is no alternative (or they are all likely to be just as bad).

10 CUSTOMER MONITORING

The final area of nonconformity to discuss is customer complaints. Because there is a strong incentive to do something in response to customer complaints, all organisations, whether they have a formal quality system or not, respond in some way to these problems. The quality assurance approach, however, is to look beyond just dealing with the immediate issue of an unhappy customer and seek to prevent or lessen the chance of the same problem arising again. A further step still is to positively monitor satisfaction rather than assume customers are happy until they complain; in other words customer related problems are actively sought out as a means to continual quality improvement. All these aspects of customer monitoring are covered in this chapter.

CUSTOMER COMPLAINTS

Dealing with customer complaints is a requirement of ISO 9000 – see *4.14.2 Corrective action*. Assessment bodies also attach considerable importance to the handling of customer complaints – more so than might be expected from the fairly brief mention given to it in the Standard. A quality manager, therefore, needs to ensure that customer complaints are dealt with effectively – the documented quality system should include procedures covering the responsibility for handling complaints and the steps to be taken when any are received. Such procedures may be separate (ie specifically covering customer complaints) or be part of more general corrective action procedures.

The first priority is to make sure that any complaints are identified and reported rather than swept under the carpet. This may not be an easy task. Whatever the culture of the organisation, there will inevitably be some desire not to wash dirty linen in public – a department, receiving a complaint about their own work, will have a natural tendency to wish to solve the problem as best they can without involving other departments or the higher levels of the organisation. Apart from anything else, there is usually an element of organisational politics involved. The quality manager needs to try and ensure that this does not happen and that all complaints, however received, are formally logged. This covers verbal complaints as well as those in writing or those implicit in returned goods or disputes over invoices. Only if this is done comprehensively can there be any confidence that complaints are being dealt with in the best way possible, including in relation to long-term prevention and quality improvement.

Achieving the necessary openness in admitting customer complaints is often a challenge for a quality manager; the organisational pressure for concealment is invariably strong. Part of the solution is bound up with the need for a problem-solving rather than a blaming culture, where complaints are seen as an opportunity for improvement rather than scapegoating. However, changing a culture is always a hard, long-term project and no quality manager can achieve this on his or her own. Apart from engineering this sort of strategic change, it is largely a matter of the quality manager actively encouraging complaint reporting and pushing staff to be positive in this respect. Complaints are also more likely to be reported internally if concealment is hard because other mechanisms are likely to identify them in the long run. The approach of positive monitoring, discussed shortly, indirectly provides such a mechanism since a concealed complaint is likely to come to light through the monitoring carried out by the quality manager or other staff not directly involved in the causes of the problem.

However reported, the first step in a customer complaint procedure is to log the complaint and cross reference it to any related documents such as an internal report of the complaint received or a letter from the customer. Such a log enables checks to be made on whether customer complaints are dealt with as well as providing data for identifying recurring problems which call for system or other structural changes. The log can take a variety of forms – it may be a separate one for complaints or it may be integrated with records of operational nonconformities or be part of corrective action records (see Chapter 11). It can be in paper form or kept as a computer file. Ideally, though, the log and records should be kept centrally by the quality manager, rather than within departments receiving the complaint; in this way the total level of customer complaints coming into an organisation can be monitored and causes sought across as well as within departments.

Logging complaints is of course only a means to an end and is definitely not a case of ISO 9000 bureaucracy. Complaints need acting on and in every case there are two levels of response to consider: firstly taking action to deal with the customer's problem (and hopefully alleviate it), and secondly addressing the long-term implications for how the organisation meets its customers' needs.

The initial response to solve the customer's problem, or at least reduce the dissatisfaction, obviously depends on a very wide range of factors, including the nature and seriousness of the problem (one component returned from a delivery of a hundred is a rather different level of problem to a complaint that a £1 million capital plant delivery fundamentally fails to meet the specification), the cost of solving it and the standing of the customer – realistically the response to a customer which accounts for half the business of an organisation will be different to a one-off, small-order customer. Also, it may be concluded that some complaints have no real basis and that the organisation is unwilling to provide a solution to please an 'unreasonable' customer; dealing with complaints inevitably has a commercial component and the cost of a solution may outweigh the loss from a dissatisfied customer. In the long term, however, dealing with problems, especially preventing them, nearly always pays off.

This immediate response to a customer complaint will in most cases, be best dealt with by the department whose problem it seems to be and usually there will be little argument about this responsibility. Also, it is quite likely that the sales department will be involved and act to ensure that some action is taken. In these cases, the role of the quality manager is likely to be fairly passive and confined to logging that effective immediate action has been taken or any other outcome. The more proactive responsibility for a quality manager, in relation to customer complaint handling, is in the second stage, considering the longer-term implications. Assuming the customer's complaint has some foundation, there must be some internal cause which produced this quality problem and the objective in this second stage of dealing with complaints is to identify the causes and find ways of preventing or reducing further occurences of this problem.

In principle, the mechanism for this second stage of handling customer complaints is the corrective action procedure and this is discussed in the next chapter. Depending on the organisation, the number of complaints received and the seriousness of the problem, it may be appropriate to deal with each complaint in this way. However, in organisations with a large customer base and many and frequent low-value deliveries, the number of complaints may overwhelm the corrective action procedure if each and every one is followed up in this way. The alternative is to treat each complaint as a minor nonconformity (like operational minor nonconformities), log them and on the basis of an analysis of the incidents over a period (eg using Pareto analysis) to select those which justify investigation through the corrective action procedure. However, the quality manager needs to exercise some judgement – if a complaint is obviously serious or possibly a symptom of an acute internal problem (eg contamination of a process), immediate, full corrective action and investigation may be urgently required. The ability and confidence to exercise this and other sorts of discretion is why being a quality manager is not just a matter of routine administration.

POSITIVE MONITORING

An assumption behind customer complaint handling is that customers will complain if they are dissatisfied and if they do not then all is well. This is simply not true. Often customers only complain (or just switch supplier) when a certain threshold of dissatisfaction is passed and well before this point they are less than content with the products or service provided to them. In other words they are passively or latently dissatisfied. When they do finally complain, their dissatisfaction level will be considerable and it may be too late to put things right – regardless of what is now done the customer decides to seek satisfactory supplies from other companies. There is, therefore, a strong case for taking action to identify and follow up latent dissatisfaction before the complaint threshold is passed. Moreover, monitoring customer satisfaction gives the opportunity to go beyond preventing dissatisfaction. Instead it is concerned with delighting customers, increasing satisfaction rather than reducing dissatisfaction.

For these reasons, we recommend that a quality system should include an element of positive monitoring. However, it should be said that this goes beyond the explicit requirements of ISO 9000; none of the clauses specifically refer to this sort of approach. Positive monitoring, though, comfortably fits into an ISO 9000 quality system and arguably relates to the fundamental point of having quality management at all – achieving quality through meeting requirements. How can you be seeking quality without knowing whether your customers *are* satisfied and their requirements met?

Despite these strong arguments for positive monitoring, many organisations are reluctant to do it. This is often rationalised as 'not wanting to bother customers'. Behind this may be some belief that it is better to let sleeping dogs lie – to contact customers may be to encourage them to find something to moan about. But this is short-sighted. Even if the customer is stimulated to look for problems, these should be seen as opportunities to excel in service and so gain a competitive advantage. Furthermore, positive monitoring gives customers the opportunity to articulate problems which are already real and evident but for one reason or another have not (yet) been raised as complaints. Nor are customers irritated by the mechanics of monitoring; nearly everyone is interested in commenting on matters which effect them directly. Being contacted in this way by a supplier is, therefore, virtually always seen as good marketing – it shows the supplier cares and values the business.

MONITORING METHODS

There are many different ways of carrying out positive customer monitoring and which is effective largely depends on the nature and size of an organisation's customer base. Consider two extremes: one is a business supplying very high-value orders to a handful of customers and the other is dealing with hundreds of thousands of final customers for low-value consumer items, distributed through a retail network. In the former case, effective monitoring may just involve informal but high-level contact between the supplier and customer; ideally, the chief executive of the supplier regularly contacting and discussing the business with his or her opposite number. A formal procedure may not be required at all to achieve this. By contrast, monitoring customer satisfaction in a large retail market is likely to be beyond the technical skills and resources of the organisation and will require the services of an outside specialist such as a market research company, although in-house monitoring of immediate customers (wholesalers or large retail chains) may be practical.

For the purposes of suggesting practical methods of positive monitoring, we shall assume that the context is an organisation with a customer base of several hundreds of customers – too many to deal with without a formal and systematic approach, but few enough to handle internally. The procedures involved may be carried out by the quality manager but often the sales or marketing function may be better placed to do the routine work, although, if this is so, the quality manager is likely to be involved as well, setting up the system and making sure it works effectively.

In most cases the easiest (and because it is more likely to be actually done, the best) method of customer monitoring is a postal survey. Once the system is designed, its administration can be delegated to quite junior staff, with the mail out initiated by simple triggers such as a copy of a delivery note or final invoice. Depending on the number of customers involved, all can be covered or just a sample contacted, but, in the latter case, those approached must be representative of the whole customer base – there is no point in just monitoring those known to be content or missing out those with known problems. Picking an effective and representative sample is not always as simple as it might appear and careful thought and possibly specialist advice may be needed. Customers (whether all or a sample) can be contacted after every delivery or, if these are frequent, at regular intervals, requesting a response on the basis of supplies received in the period. There is also the question of who specifically in the customer organisation should be contacted. Possibly the order is placed by a buying department but they may be remote from experiencing the service and others may need to be contacted instead or as well (with due regard for not offending the buying department in the process).

The material mailed to customers should include a short letter explaining the purpose of customer monitoring, stressing the aim of continually improving services and products, and a response form, as well as a pre-paid or stamped addressed envelope for the reply – it should be made as easy as possible for customers to post back. The response invited can just be an open-ended comment – 'please comment on our recent service'. However, this is usually not very effective; having to think out comments is a barrier to response. Furthermore, the analysis of such replies can be laborious and is, therefore, less likely to be carried out well.

In most cases, it is, therefore, better to invite a response to some type of satisfaction 'scale'. At its simplest this can be a one-dimensional scale, either in numerical or verbal form:

Please indicate on the following scale from '10', representing very satisfied, to '1' representing very dissatisfied, your overall level of satisfaction with our service:

| 1 | 2 | 3 | 4 | 5 | 6 | 7 | 8 | 9 | 10 |

Dissatisfied..Satisfied

---

or:

Please indicate on the following scale your overall satisfaction with our service:

☐	☐	☐	☐	☐
Very dissatisfied	Quite dissatisfied	Neither satisfied/ dissatisfied	Quite satisfied	Very satisfied

---

Customers can also be invited to add additional comments to their scale response if they wish – these give pointers to where improvement may be needed. A full example of this type of simple satisfaction monitor, together with the accompanying letter, follow at the end of this chapter.

The sophistication of scalar measurement of satisfaction can be increased by using several rather than a single dimension. Numerical scales, for example, could cover the quality of the product, adherence to delivery schedules, the follow-up service and response to queries. The advantage of such an approach is that areas of comparative strength and weakness can be identified and remedial action or just continual improvement planned. However, the more scales used, the more it is a chore to complete and the less likely it will be that customers will respond at all. Also, the dimensions may be artificial and not match up to how the customer experiences the service.

With only a modest effort, a high level of response can be expected from a postal survey of customer satisfaction. Because the subject is intrinsically relevant, the large majority of customers will take the little trouble entailed to indicate their satisfaction with the service provided. However, inevitably, some will not reply, and whether this proportion is 5 per cent or 50 per cent it is possible that these customers differ in some way to the majority who do respond. Possibly the difference is related to their level of satisfaction; non-response may indicate a high level of satisfaction or possibly the opposite. To have a complete and reliable measure, therefore, it is desirable to follow-up non-responses. A reminder letter, stressing the importance attached to establishing customer satisfaction, will certainly bring in some further responses and doing this should be easy to organise as a routine procedure. A few non-responding customers, however, will remain and to have a completely reliable measure these should be phoned and their level of satisfaction established there and then. This work can be done by the quality manager's staff or someone else, possibly even the chief executive – it shows real commitment to customer satisfaction.

Alternatively, phone methods can be used entirely instead of a postal survey and this should overcome most problems of non-response. However, with a significant number of customers to contact, phone monitoring can become a real chore and, therefore, less likely to be done regularly. Also, phoning customers requires more skill than simply sending out a postal questionnaire. Other methods of measuring satisfaction include self-completion forms accompanying the product and administration of the survey by sales or installation staff. Both have something to be said in their favour but in each case there are problems. Self-completion forms with the product usually produce fairly low responses (they may just be missed) and administered forms may not be as objective or allow enough time for customers to experience fully the product or service.

USING CUSTOMER MONITORING FEEDBACK

The results of customer monitoring can be used in two ways: to plot the organisation's overall performance and, secondly, to identify particular customers requiring individual follow-up. In both cases, the quality manager is likely to be closely involved in the work.

The aggregated responses from customer satisfaction monitoring provide a measure of an organisation's quality level and, therefore, are an important indicator of corporate health. Assuming a scale* is used, objectives can be set in terms of average satisfaction levels, eg a score of '8' (out of '10') or above, and in later years the aim may be to increase this by a determined amount. Conversely, a fall in the average score over a period may indicate some quality slippage and problems that need urgent attention. In such a case, the procedure may be to initiate a corrective action to investigate the causes and find a solution to the problems.

Processing returned forms to compute average scores should be easy and requires no special skills – the score of each response is added to a previous total and a new average calculated (ie by dividing by the total number of responses in the period). If only a single average is sought from one satisfaction dimension, the process is so simple that computerisation is probably not worth the effort. However, if several dimensions are used in the measurement and an overall average is also required (perhaps weighted by the importance attached to each dimension – see Chapter 9), mechanisation of the calculation may be desirable. Similarly, if instead of an average for all customers, averages by customer group are considered useful measures, the work involved may be enough to require more than simple clerical methods.

The other use of the responses is to identify individual cases requiring follow-up. As argued earlier, a customer may be dissatisfied but not go to

---

* If a verbal rather than numerical scale is used, the responses can of course be converted to values, eg 'very satisfied' = 10 etc.

the trouble of actively complaining. However, the occasion of responding to the satisfaction monitor may be used to highlight a problem through giving a low score, backed, perhaps, with additional comments. As a means of triggering appropriate action, the customer monitoring procedure may provide for treating a response below a certain level as a complaint leading to or feeding into corrective action, as well as requiring a direct and immediate response to the customer. Where a numerical scale is used, the triggering score might be anything under '7'. However, a lot depends on the established norms – in some organisations and circumstances a score below '8' might be thought to need action, while in others the critical level might be lower.

**BUSINESS
& MARKET
RESEARCH
— P L C —**

BUXTON ROAD, HIGH LANE VILLAGE, STOCKPORT, CHESHIRE SK6 8DX
TELEPHONE: (0663) 765115   FAX: (0663) 762362

Mr Richard Stanton
Sensormatic
1 Maxted Close
Hemel Hempstead
Hertfordshire HP2 7EG

Dear Richard

As you know we recently completed a market research survey for you. Thank you for
choosing Business & Market Research to carry out the work and we hope that we can be of
use to you again in the future.

We are very keen to make sure that our work is of good quality and that you were satisfied
with the job. We have always sent out quality control forms but now the system is a little
more formalised, as it is part of our ISO 9000 Quality System procedures. Therefore, we
would very much appreciate it if you could spare a few seconds to fill in the attached form
and return it to us in the envelope provided.

Thank you for your co-operation.

Yours sincerely

Kate Roberts
Director
19 December 1994

Enc

Registered Office as above   Registered No. 1138270 (England)

QUALITY CONTROL FORM   15 December 1994

Contact Name: RICHARD STANTON

Company: SENSORMATIC

Job: 104941 SELF SERVICE RESEARCH

Please would you rate your satisfaction with the above job on a scale of 1 to 10, where 10 is the best you can give.

1   2   3   4   5   6   7   8   9   10

Your overall comments on the job(s)

_____

_____

_____

Have you any suggestions as to how we could improve any aspect of our service to you?

_____

_____

_____

Please indicate below if you do not want us to quote your comments

_____

Please return in the enclosed Reply Paid Envelope

BUSINESS
& MARKET
RESEARCH
— P L C —

11 CORRECTIVE ACTION

The previous four chapters have discussed how problems are identified; problems found through internal auditing, monitoring operational and supplier nonconformities and those arising from customer complaints. This chapter discusses the formal process of finding long-term solutions to these problems, by means of corrective action which has a central role in a quality system as a mechanism for achieving quality improvement.

The use of the corrective action process is also a requirement of ISO 9000 (*4.14 Corrective and preventive action*). In fact, the relevant clause distinguishes two steps in the problem-solving process: corrective action (*4.14.2*) and preventive action (*4.14.3*). This distinction was made for the first time in the 1994 revision to the Standard (previously corrective action alone was referred to) and the intention is to require that a quality system should produce long-term solutions (preventive action – preventing recurrence) as well as quick-fix and short-term patching (corrective action – putting things right quickly). However, even before this revision, the need for the longer-term solution was implied in the whole concept of quality assurance and quality systems and the intention of the change was mainly to clarify this and make it explicit. For the purpose of this chapter, we shall use the term 'corrective' action to cover both 'preventive' and 'corrective' action, and the process discussed covers both requirements of the Standard.

OUTLINE OF THE CORRECTIVE ACTION PROCESS

Figure 11.1 opposite summarises the corrective action process. Corrective actions originate from and are triggered by the six sources shown as the top line of the figure. The corrective action process itself then starts with a problem from these sources being formally defined – one corrective action should address one defined problem. The causes of the problem are then investigated and on the basis of this analysis a recommendation is made for a solution which will prevent or reduce the chances of the same problem recurring. This is then considered by the organisation's management and, if thought appropriate, implementation of this recommendation is authorised. Depending on the recommendation, the quality system is then either changed or steps are taken to operate it better. There is also a third option – do nothing. In due course, the part of the quality system concerned is audited (either as part of the ongoing schedule or as a follow-up audit) and if the solution does not appear to be effective the corrective action process can be repeated until a long-term answer is found.

The steps in the corrective action process should be defined in a quality system procedure – this is a requirement of ISO 9000 – and should link this mechanism to the particular structure and needs of the individual organisation. As part of the procedure, records need to be kept to show the progress and outcome of each corrective action. An effective form of recording is to number sequentially each corrective action and keep a register or log showing which stage in the process has been reached. A form should be completed, recording in each case relevant details including the problem investigated, the recommendation made and the outcome. The staff involved in the process and dates should also be identified on the form (and perhaps in the log as well). Examples of a corrective action form and log follow at the end of this chapter.

The quality manager should be very much involved in the corrective action process and it should be his or her responsibility to make sure that corrective actions are initiated and followed through to a satisfactory outcome. The quality manager's role in this area is summarised below and each task is discussed in this chapter.

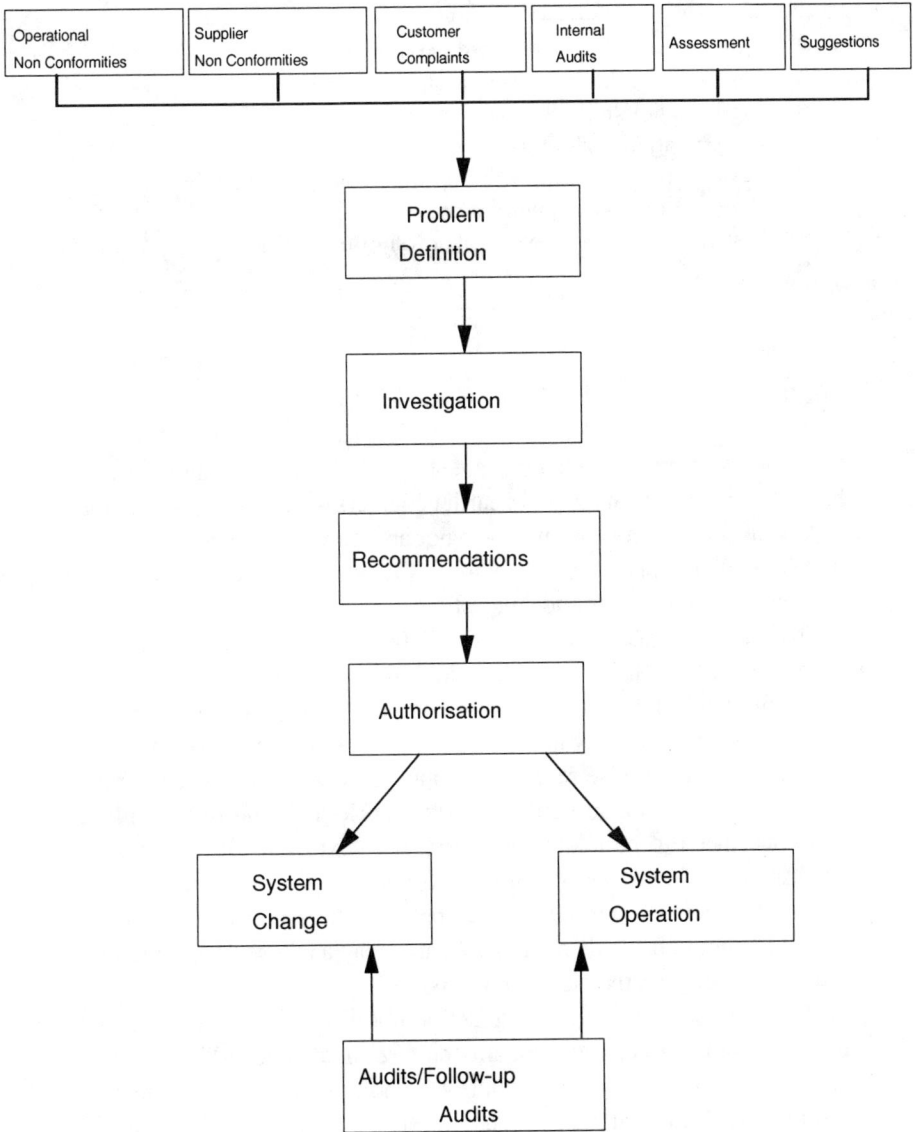

Figure 11.1 Corrective action process

Corrective actions – the quality manager's role

- Problem selection and gate-keeping
- Ensuring problems are adequately defined
- Setting a timetable
- Appointing investigators
- Reviewing, authorising or referring for authorisation the investigator's recommendations
- System change or implementing other decisions
- Auditing

ORIGINS OF CORRECTIVE ACTIONS

Six sources of corrective actions are shown in Figure 11.1. Four of these have been discussed at length in earlier chapters – internal audits (Chapter 7), operational nonconformities – major and minor (Chapter 8), suppliers (Chapter 9) and customer complaints (Chapter 10). The remaining two sources are assessments and suggestions.

If in an initial assessment to ISO 9000 or in follow-up surveillance visits the assessor finds nonconformities, the organisation concerned will be required to address and solve these problems. In the initial assessment, an effective solution may have to be found and implemented before ISO 9000 is achieved or else registration may be conditional on action being taken before the first surveillance visit (problems found in surveillance visits will need to be addressed before the next one). Other aspects of assessment and nonconformities identified in assessment are discussed later in Chapter 15, but the point to be made here is that such nonconformities should be dealt with in the same way as those found internally – through the corrective action process.

The other source of corrective action not discussed before is suggestions. A quality system and a quality culture should encourage all staff to suggest how processes can be improved and how the quality system can be changed for the better. As discussed earlier (Chapter 6), a key principle of a quality system is that procedures must be followed even if they do not appear to be effective. Where this is the case, corrective action enables suggestions for change to be investigated, evaluated and, if appropriate, implemented so that the deficiencies in the system are removed. Suggestions for change may also be made not to address a specific problem but just because there appears to be a better way of doing things – perhaps a change which anticipates problems – and these too should be formally evaluated through the corrective action process. To harness creative suggestions, the procedures and structure should enable staff, at all levels, to have access to the corrective action procedure – either directly through the quality manager or via line managers – although this does not have to mean that every single suggestion is followed up.

With six sources potentially feeding into the process, corrective actions can get out of hand with the result that either a disproportionate amount of effort is spent on them or else the whole process becomes so clogged that effective solutions are never found and implemented. Some prioritising and gate-keeping is, therefore, needed and the quality manager should either be responsible for this or ensure it happens at an earlier stage.

In discussing operational and supplier nonconformities and customer complaints we described the need for and methods of prioritisation (eg through Pareto analysis) and this may well be carried out by line managers who then pass on to the quality manager those problems where corrective action seems a priority. In this case the quality manager's role may be one of a final filter, perhaps setting more or less urgent timetables for the respective corrective actions raised. In other cases, the quality manager may well be directly involved in this prior analysis of nonconformities.

In the case of internal audit results there is normally less need to filter nonconformities into the process – all significant nonconformities identified in auditing should lead into a corrective action. However, there is the question of what is 'significant' and this will require judgement which may be exercised by the auditors or by the quality manager (ie the auditors discuss identified nonconformities with the quality manager before a corrective action is raised); the specific arrangements in this respect should be defined in the audit procedures. In the case of nonconformities identified by outside assessors, there is no room for discretion or gate-keeping – something has to be done in each case.

The quality manager also has the responsibility (and perhaps the sole responsibility) of filtering and gate-keeping staff suggestions. The right culture should generate too many suggestions to sensibly process through corrective actions and some selection is likely to be essential. However, this is a delicate task requiring sensitive handling. While the system must not be overloaded, there is a danger that rejection will disappoint staff and discourage them in future. Someone's idea may appear to be eccentric and not justify investigation, but diplomatic handling rather than curt dismissal is needed. Nor, in the long run, can all doubtful ideas be 'lost in the system'; this too will stifle the future flow of ideas.

PROBLEM DEFINITION

The first step in the corrective action process is to define the problem which is to be investigated. This should normally be done by the manager or member of staff identifying it, although the quality manager may need to assist in arriving at an effective formulation. The problem should be set out succinctly and as precisely as possible and (with the exception of suggestions) should not prejudge either the cause of the problem or imply the solution; this should be arrived at through the investigation. A couple of examples will, hopefully, illustrate these principles.

In a manufacturing process, monitoring of operational nonconformities may have indicated that an increasing proportion of components produced are out of dimensional tolerance. In this case the problem could be stated in a form such as:

The proportion of output out of tolerance from process X is rising.

The proportions, instances and timescale of this might also be detailed or this might be left as a first stage in the investigation. Notice that no assumptions are made in this case about why the rate of faults is increasing such as is implied by the next two statements of the same problem:

Why is process equipment X producing an increasing rate of out of tolerance output?

or:

Why are staff on process X producing an increasing rate of faults?

In both the above, assumptions are made about the source of the problem – the equipment or the staff – and in either case these may be wrong.

An audit may have identified that in a particular area, a procedure is not being followed. In stating the problem for corrective action it should not be assumed that the fault lies with unwilling or incapable staff. Possibly, the procedure itself is ineffective and unworkable and with the best will in the world it cannot be followed. Equally, it should not be assumed that the procedure is defective; perhaps it is down to staff retraining. Neither explanation should be prejudged.

In avoiding prejudgement in the statement of these problems, we are also avoiding allocating blame. The same principle should apply in corrective actions arising from supplier nonconformities and customer complaints. The problem may be that the product supplied was faulty but the blame may not lie entirely with the supplier – possibly the order was not placed adequately. The corrective action should investigate the various possibilities and start with a simple statement of the problem which avoids any assumptions of blame – 'Product consignment Y was defective in the following respects…' Similarly, an investigation of a customer complaint should not assume that the fault lies in a particular part of the organisation – the product may not have matched requirements because it was not adequately specified rather than it was badly made. It is also possible that the investigation will lead to the conclusion that the complaint is really groundless (although on commercial grounds the customer may still need some remedy).

The only exception to the principle that the statement of the problem should not prejudge causes or the solution is in the case of suggestions. Obviously, a suggestion contains the solution and in this case the focus of the investigation will be its evaluation.

CHOICE OF INVESTIGATOR

After the problem is defined and written down (eg on the corrective action form), the next step in the process is for the quality manager to appoint an investigator (or investigators) whose objective is to identify the causes of the problem and recommend action to provide a solution.

In many cases, the investigator should be someone other than the person or persons identifying the problem, and this is certainly the case for corrective actions arising from internal audits and suggestions. Also, nonconformities raised by assessors are obviously investigated independently. Customer complaints too are better investigated by staff not directly involved in producing the product or service concerned. However, the position is less clear-cut for operational and supplier nonconformities; the line managers or staff involved may well be best placed to find a solution.

In selecting investigators, there is a balance to strike between choosing those with relevant technical knowledge and experience of the processes covered in the investigation and bringing in a fresh point of view. Depending on the process, some technical knowledge and experience may be needed to unravel the problem and suggest practical solutions. However, the staff involved may be unable to uncover underlying causes or set aside rigid assumptions about how a process works and sometimes an outside opinion is needed. This is another area where much depends on the judgement and discretion of the quality manager.

As just discussed, we firmly recommend that the problem definition should not include assumptions about causes or solutions. However, this does not have to mean that the quality manager, in appointing the investigator, cannot make some prior judgement about possible causes or even solutions. This is particularly the case where it seems likely that the problem lies in staff not following quality system procedures, quite possibly because they simply do not know what they are supposed to do. These are the sorts of problems often identified through internal audits. Where the quality manager believes this to be the case, it may be effective to make the person not apparently following the procedure the investigator. If it is a case of not knowing the procedure, the 'investigation' should solve the problem; in carrying out the investigation the member of staff will have to find out what ought to be done. However, the investigation also gives them an opportunity to say if there is a problem in following the procedure – perhaps it is difficult to follow.

Appointing the 'culprit' as investigator can, therefore, be effective but as already mentioned (Chapter 7), this approach should be used with restraint and discretion. The corrective action procedure should not be used or seen as a disciplinary device. Staff should not be 'punished' by having to go through the chore of a corrective action every time they forget a procedure. Also, failure to follow procedures may reflect deeper problems such as a lack of training effort or a user-unfriendly procedure manual and such a wider view may need to be taken as part of the investigation.

That the corrective action procedure is not a disciplinary device should also apply to raising problems. In some organisations, corrective actions are 'raised against' other departments or staff. It is desirable that nonconformities in processes should be dealt with through corrective actions and the person reporting the problem may well believe that the source of the problem is outside his or her own area, ie lies with other staff. However, the approach should be to find causes rather than allocate blame. The appropriate investigator may be selected from the department where the problem seems to originate but the impression that the corrective action is a charge to answer should be avoided as much as possible.

A final point about selecting investigators is that the quality manager will often have to make some assumption about the scale of the problem and the work that is going to be involved. Depending on this, the investigator may be a relatively junior member of staff, a manager or a whole project team. There is also a need to set a timetable and let the investigator know when a final report is required. What is a reasonable timetable depends again on the scale of the problem and depth of likely investigation as well as the time the investigator has available. However, whatever timescale is reasonable, deadlines need setting or the process will drag on indefinitely.

THE LOGIC OF INVESTIGATIONS

Each investigation will be unique and will vary in complexity. Some will require very little time and scarcely warrant any rigorous methodology (eg where staff plainly do not understand a procedure), while others may entail detailed data collection and analysis. There is, however, a logic of investigations which can be applied to most problems:

The logic of corrective action investigations

1. Measure/quantify the problem
2. Develop hypotheses about causes
3. Select hypotheses to test
4. Test
5. Draw conclusions
6. Make recommendations

The first step is to measure or quantify the problem in some detail where this is practical (in some cases it may not be). The fault rate is going up, but by how much? Is this rise at a consistent rate? When do the faults occur? What is the cost involved? etc. Measurement of this sort may suggest hypotheses about the causes of the problem (eg when the faults occur may coincide with shift changes, an accelerating rate may suggest progressive wear of process equipment, etc) and may also help when it comes to recommendations; how radical these need to be may depend on the magnitude and seriousness of the problem.

On the basis of this quantification or otherwise, the next step is to develop hypotheses about causes of the problem, ie tentative explanations. Induction from the data collected to this stage may lead to some possible explanations of the problem but creativity and lateral thinking will also be needed.

In some cases one hypothesis may stand out as the most obvious cause and the judgement may be made that there is no need to look further. However, this decision should not be made too quickly; what is obvious is not always correct. In other cases, several hypotheses may be developed to explain the problem and it will be necessary to make some judgement on which of them is the most likely. This decision should be regarded as provisional until the selected hypotheses have been tested; if they do not stand up, others (which initially appeared less likely) can be tried.

Testing of hypotheses can take many forms. The most rigorous is to carry out some sort of controlled experiment where all conditions except the variables being tested are held constant and the expected outcome from the hypothesis compared with the actual reading. Practical forms of experiment can include running machines at different settings, altering product mixes, trying out new forms of inspection and testing, trying out different quality procedures* and very many others. However, testing may take less active forms and be little more than making informed judgements on the likely causes of the problem. Possibly, in this case, the investigator will also need to take account of the views of others. While this sort of approach is clearly less 'scientific' than more rigorous experiments, it is often in practice adequate for many problems. Ideally, in making judgements,

---

* If done in a controlled way as part of a corrective action investigation, this is the one situation where approved procedures can be set aside.

some detachment from the problem is desirable and this is why the person identifying the problem (or making suggestions) may not be the ideal investigator.

As a result of hypothesis testing, conclusions can hopefully be drawn on the causes of the problem. The final step is then to make the jump to a recommendation on how the problem can be avoided or reduced in future. In some cases, the remedy may be obvious from the cause but in others a creative leap will be needed; possibly for a given problem there may be several possible solutions. Before making a firm recommendation, further testing may be needed to evaluate or test the proposed solution. This could involve pilot projects or trying out alternative procedures.

Throughout the investigation (or before, eg when monitoring nonconformities), various numerical or statistical techniques can often be very effective. Some of these are discussed in Chapter 12.

RECOMMENDATIONS

Any recommendation that comes out of a corrective action can take one of three forms:

- recommendations to change the quality system;
- recommendations on quality system operation;
- recommendations for no change.

The first type of recommendation is self-explanatory. The cause of the problem is found to be a defective procedure (or other part of the quality system) and it is recommended that a change is made to make it more effective. The investigator should recommend what change should be made and outline, if not draft, the amendment. Such a change may be substantial (eg involve rewriting a whole section of the procedure manual) or may be only minor; soon after the system is implemented there are likely to be many such small changes needed.

Recommendations on the system operation are concerned with how staff use it or – quite likely – how they do not. It may be that the investigation concludes that a procedure that had not been followed is valid and the problem is that staff do not understand what is required of them. This sort of recommendation may lead to formal training sessions but often it is as simple as 'telling Nellie what she has to do' – if Nellie is the investigator she will have already found out what she is supposed to do. Before arriving at this sort of recommendation, however, the investigator should have considered why staff have not followed the system; possibly it is because the procedure is obscurely written or is not readily accessible. In either of these cases, some change in the system may be required (eg rewriting the procedure or making extra copies available).

The final sort of recommendation is a negative one – make no change at all – and quite often this is the best course to take. A problem such as a customer complaint may be quite serious and involve substantial costs but the investigation may conclude that no change in the quality system or its operation is likely to reduce significantly the chance of a recurrence. Possibly, the cause was a random error or misjudgement and the same set of conditions are unlikely to occur again. There is also the possibility that a change in procedures is thought likely to produce other sorts of problems at least as serious as those which are addressed. Furthermore, there is always some danger that a change will produce unanticipated problems and for this reason it may be judged better to keep the system unchanged, at least for the present. If the same problem does recur, then the need for change can be revisited.

AUTHORISATION

The investigator's recommendation should be set out in a written report (eg as part of a corrective action form or attached to it) and passed to the quality manager. The recommendation and its implementation then needs to go through a formal authorisation process. What this is should be set out in the corrective action or other procedures.

If a major change to the quality system is recommended, it will generally be considered appropriate for this to be authorised by the senior management team as a whole, usually as part of a formal management review process. This is discussed later in Chapter 13. However, since this may take some time (eg if management reviews are only held quarterly), it is common practice for this authority to be delegated to the quality manager so that he or she can use discretion (perhaps in consultation with the chief executive) on which changes should be made immediately and which should be referred to a full management review. If, for example, a corrective action identified that a record was not being kept adequately because of a poorly designed form, it would be sensible to give the quality manager the authority to make an immediate change. Where the line of such discretion is drawn is for each organisation to decide.

Where the recommendation is on the operation of the quality system rather than changing it, it is the normal practice to give the quality manager responsibility to take action (or make sure others do so) and report the outcome to the next management review. The action involved may include formal training sessions or just telling staff what is required. Sometimes, the problem may be a matter of staff compliance rather than knowledge; they know what ought to be done but choose not to do it. The quality manager is best advised to pass this sort of problem on to the line manager responsible for the staff involved.

A decision to do nothing will also in due course be reported by the quality manager to a management review. In the meantime, if the quality manager is satisfied with this recommendation, there is obviously nothing that needs to be done other than to complete the relevant records (record-keeping applies to all outcomes). Depending on the procedures, the quality manager, however, may have the authority to not accept a 'do nothing' recommendation and the same may apply to the other sorts of recommendations; the quality manager or management review may decide to take a different course to that recommended. Exceptionally this may be appropriate, but if this is a common outcome there is clearly something wrong with the investigation process. Perhaps the wrong investigators are being used.

FOLLOW THROUGH

If the decision is made to change the system, the quality manager will be responsible for getting this done. This is discussed in Chapter 14. If training or other changes in the operation of the system are needed, the quality manager may be personally involved or have to make sure that others do what is required. In both cases an entry in the corrective action records should show if and when action was taken. The final step is that the procedure or area concerned in the corrective action is audited in due course. This may be during the next scheduled audit (consulting the corrective action records, should alert the auditors to check out the specific procedure) or, if the corrective action arose from an initial audit, it will be the subject of a follow-up audit (see Chapter 7). If the audit indicates the procedure (whether revised or not) is still not working the corrective action procedure may have to be followed again. This dynamic link between corrective action and audits (and also management review) was illustrated in Chapter 7 as a 'quality triangle' (see Figure 7.1 on page 91). Taken together, these three processes should ensure that a quality system works effectively and that quality improvement is continuous.

11.4.1/1   Corrective Action Form   V1

Corrective Action Form No.		

1. STATEMENT OF DEFICIENCY

....

....

....

....

Signed:.. (Person Reporting Deficiency)   Date:..................

2. INVESTIGATION REPORT

No Change Recommended ( )   Change Recommended as Below ( )

....

....

....

....

Signed:.. (Investigator)   Date:..................

3.   REFERRAL/QUALITY MANAGER ACTION

Referral ( )   QM Action ( )

4.   PROCEDURAL CHANGE DECISION

Implement Investigator's Recommendations ( )   No Change ( )

Other Changes - As Below

....

....

....

....

5.   DATE OF CHANGE IMPLEMENTATION (IF RELEVANT)

11.4.2/1

Corrective Action Register

V1

Form No	Date Issued	Issued To	Brief Description of Deficiency	Date Returned	Investigator	Date to Invest	Date Returned	Referral/ QM Action	Procedure Change Decision	Date of Implementation (If Relevant)

STATISTICAL METHODS – USING NUMBERS

The aim of this chapter is to encourage a quality manager to use numbers and statistics as a practical tool for maintaining and improving quality. Realistically, we cannot in the space of a few pages describe in any detail the many or even just some of the techniques which are available and we urge the reader to follow up this brief taste of what statistics can achieve by referring to other books. There are many sources available on using numbers and statistics in quality mangagement; as a starter we can recommend two – Price and Taguchi (see the bibliography). Also, as part of leading the reader into this area we have another agenda: reducing the fear of statistics – which is often why they are not used at all.

STATISTICS – WHERE MORTALS FEAR TO TREAD

Figure 12.1 illustrates the common problem with statistics; it appears to be all about arcane techniques, which might as well be in the language of another universe for anyone whose formal mathematical education finished at sixteen or so.

When the words 'statistics' is used, the image is that of the complex formula in Figure 12.1. Many potential users, having this outlook, are frightened off by such an apparently daunting subject and are never likely to get involved willingly to find whether it offers any practical management benefits (it is safer to assume it does not!). A manager may get by with this attitude until the arrival of ISO 9000 onto the scene. The last clause of the Standard (*4.20 Statistical techniques*) sets out a requirement for 'identifying the need for statistical techniques required for establishing, controlling and verifying process capability and product characteristics'. Many organisations developing a quality system to ISO 9000 at this point run for cover. And there is an escape route; if you cannot identify any need for such statistical techniques you do not have to struggle to use them. So, it is common to put forward a case that there are no areas of the operation that could use this type of technique and, therefore, this section of the Standard does not apply. What a relief! Other organisations, where this argument cannot be sensibly defended to assessors, half-heartedly apply some form of statistical methods on a token and minimal basis in order satisfy the Standard; nothing useful is expected from this busy work and of course nothing is achieved. As we have indicated elsewhere, doing something just to meet ISO 9000 is a bad reason for doing anything, let alone something as potentially useful as the concept of working with numbers.

$$S^2 = \frac{1}{n} \sum_{i=1}^{n} (x_i - \bar{x})^2$$

Figure 12.1   Statistical formula

Working effectively with numbers rather than forcing reluctant managers to take up a new subject from scratch is the real concept behind this part of ISO 9000. It should be seen as a prompt by the Standard to think seriously whether some sort of numerical techniques can provide a tool for controlling processes, monitoring the output and solving problems. The maxim 'if you can't measure it, you can't manage it' has a lot of validity. The real barrier is that the ISO 9000 road has the daunting sign 'statistics' and this tends to turn back all but the most determined of travellers. If the sign said something more friendly and less alarming such as 'working with numbers' many more organisations would realise that they do not need to bring PhD level statisticians onto the payroll in order to start using the sort of tools behind 'statistical techniques'.

STARTING AT THE GROUND FLOOR – USING NUMBERS

There are many statistical formulae such as that in Figure 12.1 and they do have a role to play in working numerically. However, they represent a far point on a spectrum of techniques which range from the very simple that almost anyone can use, to those which are complex and require real technical skill and training. Luckily, though, the simplest methods are often capable of yielding the largest proportion of possible benefits. The difficult and complex have a place but not in the large majority of normal business applications. This important fact is just not realised by the many organisations which are managed by the statistical refugees we have already mentioned.

The value of even simple numerical methods can best be demonstrated by an example of the use of basic numbers to investigate a typical process problem which requires a solution – speeding up the time taken to carry out design work. The case we have in mind involves four sub-processes, each of which covers allocated tasks. Figure 12.2 illustrates this.

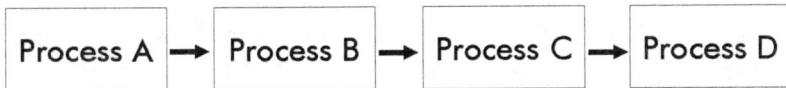

Process A → Process B → Process C → Process D

Figure 12.2 Process flow

When facing the problem of improving the overall time of the design process, many would use 'common sense' and their knowledge of the tasks involved to decide that the thing to do is to add extra resources (more staff, a new computer, etc) to, say, process B and that is that, end of problem. This may sound simplistic but it is used all too often, especially where there are vested interests, eg the manager of process B *wants* a new computer.

However, without any real knowledge of the previous situation, how can the new proposal be evaluated after it has been carried out? Better perhaps not to jump at a solution yet but to gather some information. This could be done by measuring the performance of each part of the process over a period of time. Suppose the results shown in Figure 12.3 (opposite) were obtained.

This now shows the process and transfer times, and by adding them together, overall processing takes 18 hours. Process B does seem to be the largest consumer of time so perhaps the new computer is the right answer after all. Suppose further investigation indicated that the computer would cost £10,000 and would reduce the time by 1 hour. Good news for manager B? An alternative approach, however, relates to transfer times. This takes up six hours, a third of the whole process time and larger than that of any sub-process. Investigations into this area indicate that reorganising transfer (which would have zero cost) can save three hours. Such a solution could be implemented quickly and the improvement demonstrated. If it works then the target has been met. If not then other ideas could be tested in a similar way.

None of this could be regarded as high level mathematics and need not carry the frightening label of 'statistics'. Yet this approach, simplistic though it is, is based upon an actual case which yielded significant benefits for the company involved to the delight of all (except manager B).

There are an infinite number of ways in which such simple numerical analysis can aid practical management. In other chapters of this book we have suggested a few applications such as using very simple scoring methods to manage suppliers (see Chapter 9) or monitor customer satisfaction (Chapter 10). These too require no more than basic numeracy. Also, the Pareto curve analysis discussed in Chapter 8 may sound more forbidding, but in practice involves little more than sorting, counting and drawing a simple chart. Yet it offers an effective way of setting priorities for quality improvement. Let us now go further and see how numerical methods can address problems in the areas specifically mentioned in the Standard.

CAN WE DO IT? – PROCESS CAPABILITY

Moving beyond the simplest use of numbers to investigate problems, we come to a set of techniques which are a little more involved in 'real' statistics. These involve the concept of *variation* to investigate how processes can be investigated and controlled.

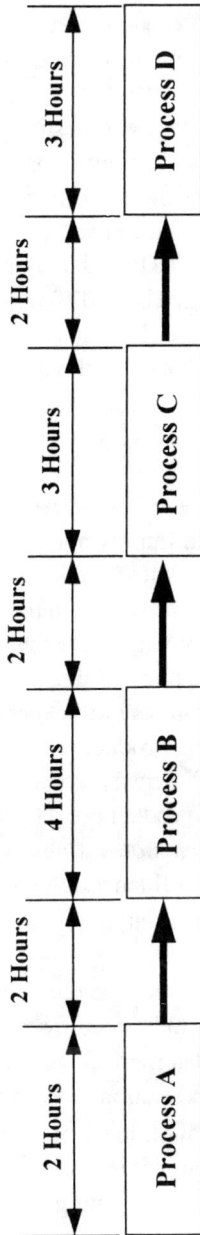

Figure 12.3 Process flow, with information

No two things in the universe are *absolutely* identical – they are never the same in every single respect. Two objects may appear similar but, if investigated deeply enough, will show differences – there will be variation. Take this page as an example. If we were to go to six points at random and measure the page thickness with a suitably accurate device, it would be apparent that the thickness varies across and along the page. Is this a problem? Does it matter? Almost certainly it does not. Despite this variation, the printer has been able to use the paper in the printing process to produce the book. So obviously this amount of variation is not a problem. However, things could have been different. Had the thickness variation been greater, this could have prevented the printing operation. So the question relating to the paper thickness should not be 'does it vary?' because the answer to that will always be yes, but 'how much does it vary?' or perhaps even better 'how much can it vary before the printing process becomes difficult or even impossible?'

The concept of variation underlies many of the statistical techniques used within quality management and improvement. Continuing with the example of paper, the variation in thickness is due to many factors during its manufacture. These could be, say, variations in the raw materials, very minor differences in mix consistency within a batch, slight vibrations in the production equipment, etc. Some or all of these and other factors will combine together to produce the changes in thickness. The same is true of any other process and the resulting product will display the same sort of variability in its properties (length, density, colour, etc.). The same can also apply to a service rather than a product process. These slight differences are known as the *normal* or *common* variability of a process. This implies that left alone, with no other influences, the process will continue to produce this level of variation in the output (eg thickness varying by ± x per cent).

If customer requirements are to be met – and quality is to be achieved – the normal variation of the process must be known *and* this must not be greater than the variation that the customer can accommodate – a printer may be happy with paper thickness variations within a tolerance of, say, ± 0.001 mm. Discovering the maximum level of normal variability and comparing it with the customer requirements (usually expressed in the form of a specification) is known as establishing the *process capability*, a term that is used in the Standard.

Information about process capability is a very valuable tool. With this knowledge, the whole of the process can be operated with a degree of confidence concerning the outcome. There can be three possibilities if the process capability is compared with the specification. These are shown in Figure 12.4: the process variation may be greater (process A in the figure), equal to (process B) or less than (process C) the specification.

If the process produces products which vary by too great an amount (ie outside the specification, as in A), there will always be rejected products which will have to be removed, a wasteful and expensive activity that is rarely totally effective. Any rejects that are missed will result in problems for the customer and subsequently worse problems for the supplier. Given this situation, there is probably a need to change the plant or find customers with a less tight specification which is within the process capability of this plant. Or perhaps this is just the wrong business to be in.

If the maximum process variation exactly matches the specification (as in process B), then the products will be acceptable. However, this situation will only apply for as long as nothing else happens to add to the normal variation. But things do add to the normal variation. Changes in supplier, changes in batches of raw materials, shift changeovers, etc, are all potentially sources of additional variation. These factors, known as *special variations*, increase the total variation in the product and are often a cause of rejects, especially if the process capability (the normal variation) too closely matches the specifications – there is no room to accommodate anything extra. This is a recipe for continuous problems.

Finally, the maximum normal process variation may be far smaller than the range required in the specification (as in C). In this case, the special variations mentioned above would have to have a very marked effect upon the process before rejects could be produced and we might be reasonably confident that the chances of this happening are quite low. This is a healthier situation, although monitoring may still be needed to check that things do not change to the point where the variation set in the specification is approached or exceeded.

It is surprising how often organisations accept specifications from customers without any real knowledge of whether their own capability matches what is required. The use of variation techniques can avoid all the problems of promising to do something which is not possible. If the

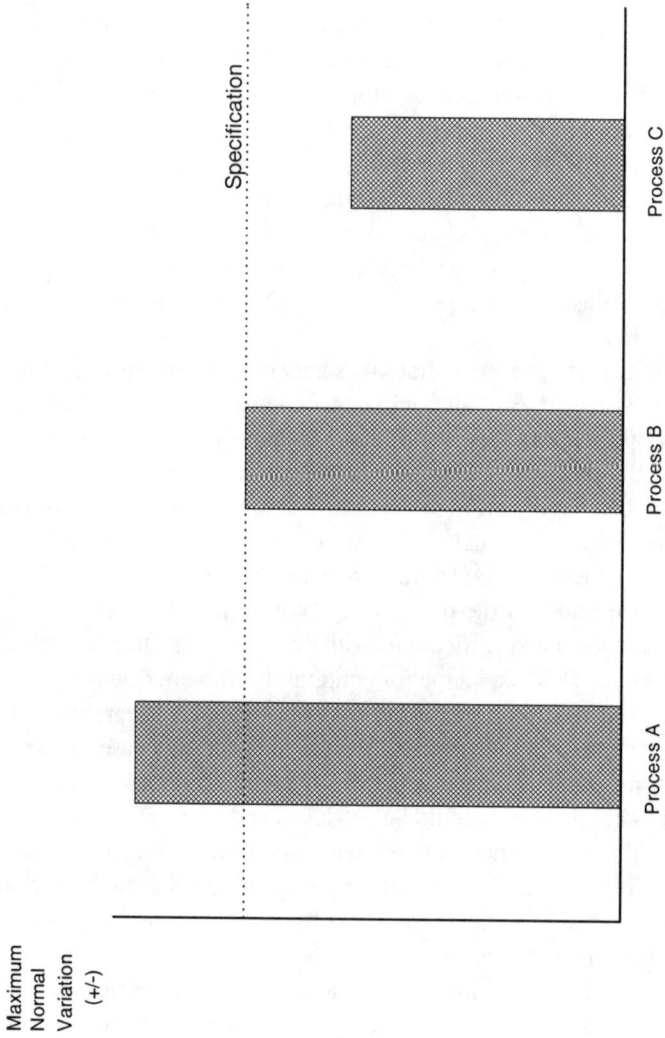

Figure 12.4 Process capability compared to a specification

process is not capable of meeting the specification it will usually be better in the short run to turn the work away. In the longer run there may be a need to upgrade capabilities to meet the market's demand. Process capability needs reviewing from time to time – how can this be done unless it is first known? The practical methods of establishing process capability will vary from process to process but in principle it is a matter of defining which process characteristics are significant (those relating to the specification) and taking sufficient measurements to establish their normal variation. Charting them is a very useful aid in this.

KEEPING AN EYE ON THINGS – PROCESS MONITORING

Having defined process capability, the next stage is to use statistics to monitor the output of the process to ensure that it remains within the specifications and, if not, to use the data to assist in subsequent investigations to identify (and possibly eliminate) the causes of special variations. These applications of statistics are, therefore, methods of monitoring operational nonconformities (as per Chapter 8) and a possible tool of the corrective action investigations discussed in the last chapter.

Let us assume that a process has been set up (eg to print books), its normal (or common) variations are known and it is making a product that it is well capable of producing, ie as per the third of the situations described above. However, as with any process, other special sources of variation will occur. This will cause the overall variation of the output to change. Examples could be those indicated above such as changes in supplier, changes in batches of raw materials, shift changeovers or any other factor which could change the variation of the process. Statistical techniques can be used to monitor the process in order to detect this change before any rejects are made.

The use of Shewhart charts – see Figure 12.5 – is one method of analysing data drawn from taking samples (eg of books) at intervals and recording their relevant measures (eg page margin spacing). The data is charted and also on the chart is noted the levels of variation that would normally be expected from the process (ie the previously established process capability). Any point that occurs outside the horizontal normal variation lines can be readily identified as being in some way related to a 'special' event.

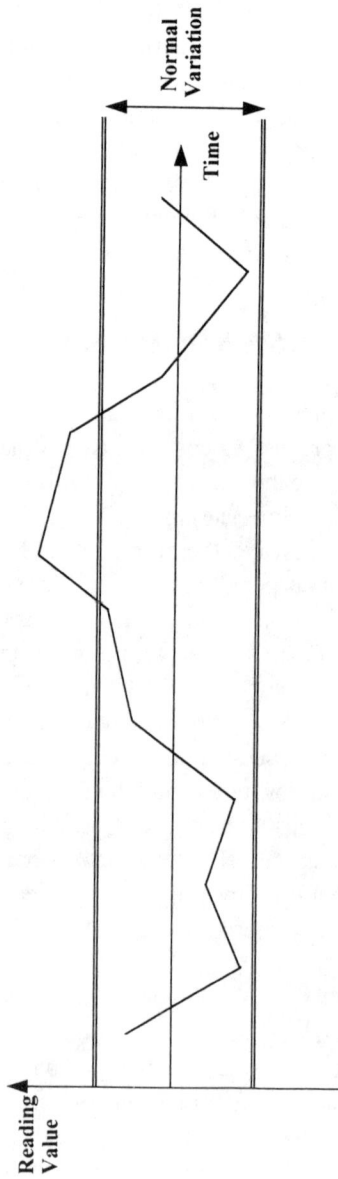

Figure 12.5 Example of control (or Shewhart) chart

Note that the horizontal lines in the chart indicate the level of normal variation, *not* that set by the specification (which will be outside these limits if we assume the process has been established to be capable). If the charting is done immediately the measurements are made (computers can facilitate this), it is possible to detect problems, investigate and correct them before any rejected product is made, ie before the total variation exceeds the specification.

The technique has another advantage. By knowing the normal variation, it is a simple matter to separate which points on the chart are within this normal range and so *should not* lead to any alteration to the system (eg turn up the speed, increase the feed-rate, etc) from those which are outside the range. The latter do call for action to bring things back to the normal. Without this sort of measurement and analysis the process operators may adjust the process unnecessarily. Such an adjustment is not only not needed but itself becomes another potential source of special variability – the action may create more problems than it solves. This would be a case of quality management without adequate measurement.

These are just a couple of practical applications of Shewhart charts. These and related techniques are often referred to as statistical process control or SPC. Despite forbidding names (such as Shewhart charts) these methods are really quite simple tools and well within the skills of anyone with basic arithmetic.

MAKING THINGS BETTER – PROCESS IMPROVEMENT

The above techniques can also be used as the start of process improvement. Having identified that some special variation has taken place, the charts provide information for use during subsequent investigation (ie corrective actions) to find the source of the problem. For example, if the same fault always occurs 30 minutes after a shift changeover, the procedures for handing over control from one shift to another would be a good place to start the investigation. In one real example, the source of a problem was tracked down to an ingredient used, at about the same time each day, in a spray cleaner in the vicinity of a chemical deposition process. In a similar fashion, batches of raw material giving increased variation can be isolated, the reasons for the problems identified and the corresponding purchase specification suitably amended.

In principle, charting should also indicate when the range of variation has decreased so allowing the causes of this positive effect to be identified and repeated. However, Murphy's law always seems to lead to changes making things worse rather than better and beneficial causes are less common than the opposite.

Another way of making improvements to the process is to examine all the elements that combine together to make up the normal variation of the process. Up until now it has been suggested that this is not an area that can be improved upon – the process is either capable (to meet the specification) or it is not. However, there are techniques (eg Taguchi methods – see bibliography – which again are not too far along the spectrum of complexity) that can assist in identifying which of the factors involved in the normal variation predominate, so that their influence can be reduced. This leads, through a series of controlled experiments, to reducing the normal variation. The consequences of this include possibly taking on orders with a tighter specification (higher quality work in the more traditional sense) or reducing the level of monitoring needed for the process. The reason why the latter may be possible is that the gap between the new lower range of normal variation and the unchanged, but now comparatively greater, variation of the specification is large enough to assume that total process variations approaching those allowed have become less likely.

So the use of simple numerical techniques (you do not have to use the term 'statistics') can lead to real improvements. The classic progression is to start with a determination of the capability of the process in question – what are its normal variations. If it is capable of meeting the specification (ie it is 'in control') consider some form of regular monitoring. The frequency of this should depend on how 'capable' the process is – if it is 'just capable' very frequent monitoring is required, but if it is 'very capable' the level needed will be less. If the process is not capable – not within the specification and 'out of control' – consider methods of bringing the process under control by identifying sources of special variation (which may be included in your process capability assessment) or by some other method such as Taguchi's.

MANAGING STATISTICS

Hopefully, this chapter (together with further reading) will have suggested where numbers and statistics might be applied effectively in terms of ISO 9000, identifying the need for statistical techniques. A quality manager, in conjunction with other managers, can review the operation and probably find practical and useful applications. The Standard also has another requirement in relation to statistics – developing procedures for using these techniques. What is required here is to document how the data (and which data specifically) required for statistical analysis should be collected and recorded and the methods (eg Shewhart charting) which will be used to process it. Guidelines are also needed on what is to be done with the results of the analysis – there is no point whatever in developing statistical methods if effective action is not taken on the output. These procedures need documenting, either in a special set of statistical technique procedures or as part of or linked to other procedures (eg those controlling processes or corrective action). Responsibilities also need defining: who is to record data and who is going to carry out the analysis and draw conclusions? In turn this will require training to be organised, although, as we hope we have shown, this does not have to mean a course of statistical theory.

13 MANAGEMENT REVIEW

Management review is a tangible form of the commitment of an organisation's management to quality assurance and its quality system. It should not be the only form this commitment takes but, carried out properly, it is an important mechanism for translating good intentions into positive action. Surprisingly, some organisations which invest considerable time and money in developing a quality system fail to carry out management review effectively with the consequences that the full benefits of the system are never realised. Management review in some form or other is an essential part of a quality system and is a requirement of ISO 9000 (clause *4.1.3 Management review*).

This chapter discusses the objectives of management review and how in practice it can be carried out. As will be shown, the quality manager has important roles in this process. However, one reason why management review is essential is that the quality manager cannot shoulder the whole responsibility for the quality system. The whole point is to involve the organisation's management team as a whole.

MANAGEMENT REVIEW OBJECTIVES

There are four key objectives of management review:

1. review the working of the quality system;

2. consider problems identified through the quality system;
3. agree and authorise changes in the system;
4. agree and authorise other changes which may be appropriate.

The review of the working of the system has three components: firstly, whether the system is working in its own terms and especially whether the procedures are being followed; secondly, whether the system is continuing to meet the Standard; and finally, but most important of all, whether the objectives of the system are being achieved.

Whether the system is working in a formal sense – ie are the procedures being followed? – should be evident from internal auditing, and reports of this activity (and from outside assessment) should be considered at review meetings. In addition, however, the review meeting should include most senior line managers and they should know how well the system is functioning in their own areas of the organisation.

One of the functions of management review specified in the Standard is to consider whether the system continues to meet the requirements of ISO 9000. However, in practice, this subject is unlikely to be an urgent concern at most review meetings. At the start, the system is developed to match the Standard and any unforeseen deficiencies in this respect will become apparent at the assessment, if not before. Such problems will then have to be discussed and addressed. As time goes on, changes will be proposed to the system, and before at least major changes are authorised, the match against ISO 9000 should be considered. Similarly, if the Standard is revised (as in 1994) changes may be needed in the system to bring it into line. As the 'expert', the quality manager should advise management in these areas but it is important that the whole team considers and shares responsibility for decisions which have a bearing on the requirements of ISO 9000.

The most important aspect of reviewing the workings of the quality system is whether its objectives are being realised. These should be set out in the quality policy but there is rather more to this part of the review than a form of words. As discussed in Chapter 3, some tangible benefits should be sought from a quality system approach. These may be in terms of customers – increasing their satisfaction – or efficiency in its various forms, and if at all possible, specific targets should be set and their attainment monitored and measured. Discussion of whether or not the objectives are being met can then deal in facts rather than just feelings and opinions.

The problems that need to be considered in management review are those discussed in earlier chapters. Specifically, those shown in Figure 11.1 in a previous chapter as the sources of corrective actions – operational and supplier nonconformities, customer complaints and findings from internal audits and outside assessment – are all relevant. Suggestions for improvements can also be regarded as 'problems'. The corrective action process and especially its recommendations – the proposed solutions to the problems – are also essential subjects at management review. This then leads on to the other two objectives of review: agreeing and authorising changes to the quality system or taking other action. Often this is a matter of considering the solutions proposed by the corrective action investigator and these may include making a change to some part of the quality system or to how it is implemented. Depending on the discretion allowed to the quality manager, some of these changes may have already been implemented in the period between management review meetings and now is the occasion for these to be formally reported. The quality manager is, as we shall discuss, likely to be primarily responsible for implementing the change decisions which are made at the review. Finally, in considering and taking other action, the management review may well take a wider view than the 'system' and look at other methods of achieving and enhancing quality. In particular, these are likely to relate to staff motivation and 'hearts and minds' issues. There is also the matter of how well the organisation communicates its quality commitment to the outside world, and in this area management review touches on marketing.

REVIEW MEETING MEMBERS

The review meeting must represent, if not include, all the senior management of the organisation (or the part of it covered by the quality system). In particular, the chief executive officer, whatever his or her title, ought to attend most, if not all, meetings and his or her absence is probably an indication of a lack of commitment to quality and the quality system. Other managers should include those heading up most of the functional areas covered by the system; more than anyone else they should know how well the system is working. Apart from senior managers, others may be invited to attend regularly or occasionally. These staff could include technical specialists. Obviously, the quality manager must attend.

In many smaller and medium-sized companies the management review is carried out by the directors (who are often responsible for nearly all management roles). In this situation, it may be appropriate to make the review part of regular board meetings provided there is enough time to cover all the topics adequately (as well as the other agenda of the board meeting). It is recommended that in this case separate minutes of the review are prepared since they may need circulating to those who might not have access to other matters discussed at board level (internal auditors and outside assessors, among others, need to see the records of management reviews).

Members of the review meetings clearly need to know that they are required to attend and also when and where the meeting will take place. The quality manager should facilitate this – eg by circulating an agenda. There is no specific requirement in the Standard to have written procedures covering management reviews but they are often useful. These can specify who is expected to attend as well as the other details of the meetings discussed shortly.

REVIEW MEETING FREQUENCY

The Standard requires review meetings to be held at 'defined intervals' but does not specify what these should be. Much will depend on the organisation and how it works, but meetings held less frequently than every quarter are unlikely to be often enough to manage the system effectively (or meet the requirements of the assessors). Many organisations will consider that monthly meetings are needed, although in each quarter two of these might be shorter and one rather longer and more comprehensive. An important point is that frequent management reviews are particularly needed when the system is first implemented, ie between start-up and assessment. Initial problems in the operation of the system are almost inevitable and these need to be considered and action agreed as soon as possible.

The formal interval between review meetings needs to be defined in the quality system documentation, either in the quality manual or in the management review meeting procedure if one is prepared. It is common and sensible practice to set a minimum interval, eg every quarter, but to hold them more often if necessary. In initial assessment or surveillance visits, outside assessors will almost always want evidence (eg meeting minutes) that the meetings have been held at the defined intervals.

MEETING PROCEEDINGS AND AGENDA

The meeting should be run in a formal way although this does not necessarily preclude full and lively discussion; the meeting needs substance and should not be held just as a matter of form to meet ISO 9000. The formality should include having a chairperson, a meeting secretary and a formal agenda.

The chairperson will often be the chief executive but other members of the review can equally take on the job if they show an aptitude for controlling meetings. The chair can also be rotated between meetings. The quality manager usually acts as meeting secretary and for this reason is disqualified from also acting as chairperson. However, if someone else takes the minutes, etc, the quality manager can take the chair.

The meeting needs information on various aspects of the working of the quality system and this can be most efficiently done by the quality manager presenting a formal report on what has happened since the last review meeting. To save time it may be better to submit this report, in writing, in advance of the meeting. A suggested scope of such a report is indicated below:

Scope of quality manager's report to management review meeting

- Results of operational nonconformity reviews.
- Results of supplier reviews or monitoring.
- Review of customer complaints received and results of customer satisfaction monitoring.
- Audits carried out and their results.
- Results of external assessments.
- Corrective actions raised, completed or underway.
- Corrective action recommendations authorised by the quality manager.
- Changes made to the quality system since the last review meeting.
- Monitoring or measurement of quality system benefits.

All this may suggest a lot of work for the quality manager and a long document. However, the report should only be a bare-bones factual report and a couple of pages should suffice. Also, the topics cover many of the key roles of the quality manager and a formal summary of what has been done is well worthwhile even if just for the quality manager's own satisfaction. The report can be attached to the meeting minutes – there is obviously no point in writing out the same thing twice over.

The other subjects of the review meeting, apart from receiving the quality manager's report, are indicated in the suggested agenda set out below. A formal agenda will ensure that everything of importance is covered and it can be circulated beforehand, although this might not be neccesary if it is the same for each meeting.

Management review meeting agenda

---

1. Date, time and members of the meeting.
2. Minutes of the last meeting.
3. Points arising from 2.
4. Report from the quality manager.
5. Working of the quality system.
6. Customer comments.
7. Corrective action recommendations referred for authorisation.
8. Agreed changes and other action relating to the quality system.
9. Other quality issues.
10. Action arising from the meeting.

Much of the suggested agenda is hopefully self-explanatory. The report from the quality manager would cover the subjects listed earlier; as well as forming a record of activities it should lead into a general discussion of the working of the quality system (item 5). The latter should include an assessment of how well the overall quality objectives are being met and the quality manager's report should include any monitoring or measures relevant to this. Customer comments, and especially complaints, should be covered in the quality manager's report but the subject is so important that it ought also to be covered separately. If positive monitoring is not used, line managers closest to customers can at least give their view on customer satisfaction levels over and above what is indicated by complaints (or their absence). Any corrective action recommendations which have not already been authorised should now be discussed and a decision made on what is to be done. The meeting should also be aware of recommendations authorised by the quality manager (or in any other ways); the quality manager's report should have covered this. This then leads on to decisions to change the quality system or implement the system in a different way, eg through training activities. The meeting can then be broadened to take in quality issues which are not directly system related. Finally, the meeting should conclude with agreement on who is responsible for making the decisions happen. Inevitably, the quality manager is likely to be most involved but other managers may well have their own roles to play as well.

MANAGEMENT REVIEW RECORDS

ISO 9000 requires that records should be made of management reviews and assessors will wish to examine these. In practice, this means taking minutes of the meetings and even if the Standard did not require this, some sort of record is essential – how else can you know what has been decided and who is responsible for taking action?

Minutes are the better for being shorter – they are more likely to be read. Decisions taken should be recorded so that no one is in any doubt. The 'collective' view of the meeting can also be summarised – eg on the workings of the quality system – but a record of what each person said at the meeting is not really necessary. If, however, there is a major split in opinion on important issues, the different views should be recorded.

Once prepared, copies of the minutes can be circulated, preferably with action points highlighted. The quality manager should keep each set of minutes in order and available for inspection by assessors and internal auditors (the management review process should itself be audited as it is a part of the quality system). It is good practice for the minutes to be formally approved at the next meeting and signed by the chairperson.

CARRYING OUT DECISIONS

The quality manager will have a major responsibility for carrying out the decisions of the management review meeting. This will include making any changes to the documented quality system and this is discussed in the next chapter. The quality manager may also be involved in changing how the quality system is implemented, including organising or leading training sessions. However, other managers should also be involved in this as well, eg coaching their own staff who are having problems following the system. The quality manager, however, may need to chase up other managers to make sure that they do whatever they have agreed.

14 CHANGING A QUALITY SYSTEM

No matter how well planned and implemented, a quality system will need to change sooner or later. Immediately after it is first brought into use, some amendment of the system will be needed to correct initial drafting and similar faults, but even when this has been done, change will continue to be necessary. We discuss shortly why this is the case. Change of a quality system is, therefore, both possible and essential. However, it must be carried out in a formal and effective way to avoid any breakdown of the document control principle discussed in Chapter 6. The quality manager has the responsibility for this and in this chapter we give some practical advice on how to make smooth changes to a quality system.

THE NEED FOR CHANGE

There are four major reasons why a quality system will need to be changed:

1. to do something better;
2. to do new things;
3. to do less things;
4. to match changes in the Standard.

The something which may be done better can include the system itself, the underlying processes it controls or the way the organisation is structured. Improvements to the system are typically to deal with deficiencies identified and analysed through corrective actions – see Chapter 11. One outcome (but not the only one) of a corrective action is a recommendation to change a defective procedure or other part of the system.

Procedures are written to match particular processes and if these change it may well be necessary to amend the related procedure; if a new piece of process plant is installed the old procedure covering this stage may now make no sense at all. Such changes to the processes may be to improve operating efficiency (perhaps to overcome problems identified through operational nonconformity monitoring) or because the product being processed is changed in some way. Similarly the organisational structure may be changed so that things work better and this, in turn, may need a change in a procedure developed to match what existed before.

A growing, or even just a surviving, organisation will also need to do many sorts of new things. These include adding new products to the range and possibly new processes to produce them. Similarly, new parts may be added to the organisation either through organic growth – eg a marketing department may be created, or new branches, or a switch to in-house manufacturing, etc – or by acquisition of other organisations. In all these cases, it may be considered necessary to add new procedures or other parts to the quality system to cover and control the expanded operations. It may also be decided that, although the processes and organisation have not been increased, additional procedures are required to ensure better control; possibly a process had no or minimal procedures to cover it and problems have been found which it is believed can be prevented by a defined procedure. However, a word of warning: there is a danger that for these and similar reasons the quality system will just grow and grow and become more and more complex. The more of it there is, the greater the chance of it breaking down. Very careful judgement is therefore needed and the quality manager should give advice and leadership in this respect. If every year the procedure manual gets thicker and thicker, the quality manager is probably not doing at least one part of his or her job adequately.

Conversely, organisations often reduce their activities and scope; product lines and associated processes are dropped, activities are contracted out or outsourced and the organisation rationalised or downsized. All this may mean that some parts of the quality system are no longer relevant to the operation and can be taken out. Also, it may be considered that some procedures serve no useful purpose even though the related activity remains; they may be found to have no practical impact on quality so why keep them in the system? Arguably all procedures should be regularly reviewed in this way. However, assuming the system is assessed to meet ISO 9000, it is important to consider whether the pruned system will still meet the Standard. It may, for example, be considered that design review procedures really achieve little or nothing but a system meeting the Standard must include this activity. Again, the major responsibility here is with the quality manager who should have enough understanding of ISO 9000 to make a reasonable judgement or at least know where to seek advice.

The three reasons already discussed for changing a quality system should all produce some real benefits to the organisation; things should be better after the change than before. The same cannot be said for the fourth reason why a quality system may need changing – to match revisions to the Standard. In this case the change is needed to keep ISO 9000 registration and most organisations are bound to see this as an unproductive nuisance. Since it was first published in 1979 (then as BS 5750), the Standard has been revised twice: in 1987 and 1994. Another change is likely around the year 2000. The 1994 revision was, arguably, more a matter of form than substance and most registered organisations have not needed to make any really substantial changes to their procedures or other parts of their quality system. Almost certainly, however, they will have had to make cosmetic changes such as redrafting their quality policy and manual and this will not have brought any tangible benefits. It is easy, though, to complain about ISO 9000 bureaucracy. If the Standard never changed it would ossify and become out of date. The 1994 revision may not have introduced any new and effective quality mechanisms but, if nothing else, it is certainly easier to read and understand. This is at least to the benefit of organisations introducing the Standard for the first time. The 1987 revision did introduce some effective changes from which many organisations have derived benefits (eg internal auditing) and future revisions may also have a positive impact.

In summary, quality systems have to change either so that they continue to match the environment in which they work or to translate into practice that commitment to quality improvement which should underlie the system. A system that never changes is almost certainly not effective, or not as effective as it could be. Assessors take this view and regard change as a positive sign, while a system which remains the same year after year is more likely to be seen as deficient than perfect.

KEEPING CONTROL

So change of the system is inevitable. This change, however, must be controlled or it will produce more problems than it solves. The quality manager has a special responsibility in this respect.

An essential feature of a quality system is uniformity – all who are required to follow a procedure must follow the same version of that procedure. It is no good if half the company work to version one and the other half to version two; quite possibly the activities will simply not fit together any more. The principle of controlled documentation, as discussed in Chapter 6, if implemented effectively, will avoid these problems. Controlled documentation, and keeping it controlled, becomes particularly essential when a system is changed. It is then that the danger of two versions being followed becomes acute. The change, therefore, needs to be carried out in such a way that a new version is substituted for all the old ones (which are then removed from use) and from some point in time all staff work to the new rather than the old procedure. Usually the change involves only part of the quality system (eg a specific set of procedures) but this can make the problems more rather than less severe.

Document control is part of making sure this all happens in the right way and we next discuss some practical mechanisms for achieving this. There is also something more that is required and this is discussed later ('letting everyone know').

CHANGE MECHANISMS

How changes are to be made to a quality system needs to be defined within the system – a procedure for document control and change. This is a requirement of ISO 9000 (*4.5 Document and data control*). The details of the mechanisms built into procedures will differ between organisations depending on their structure and mangement. However, effective change procedures need to include four elements:

1. authorisation;
2. document drafting;
3. document printing;
4. document distribution.

The quality manager will be directly involved in all the tasks that comprise these mechanisms.

Having document control and maintaining it means that any change must be authorised in an agreed and defined way. There is obviously no control if any department or other grouping can make changes to the system as and when they see fit (although they should be able to *suggest* changes for consideration and authorisation). The details of authorisation can vary but in most organisations approval of changes to the quality system will be reserved for management reviews or delegated to the quality manager (who may have discretion to approve urgent changes).

In Chapter 11 we discussed authorisation of recommended changes arising out of the corrective action process. Changes can in principle be authorised in other ways (eg a management review may consider a change which has not been suggested through the corrective action process). However, we recommend that it is better to require all changes to be formally the result of a corrective action and, therefore, each revision can be traced back to a specific corrective action. Not only is this tidy but it enables the reason for the change to be subsequently identified and this may be important, for example if the new procedure proves to be less than effective. It is surprising how quickly things such as why a change was made can be forgotten if they are not recorded in a formal way. And following the principle of all change through corrective action is not any real burden, even if occasionally it is a bit artificial, eg the corrective action record follows rather than precedes the decision to make the change.

Any change recommendation of a corrective action may have been specific about how the procedure or other part of the system should be changed, eg a draft of the proposed revision. In other cases, however, the quality manager will need to do the drafting and in any case should check others' wording before final printing. The style and formatting of the revised draft should match the original version and the rest of the system.

In Chapter 6 we discussed techniques to improve document control such as version numbering and document lists (which are usually included with each set of procedures). Together, these identify which is the most up-to-date version of a procedure etc and that this is the version in circulation. These become particularly important when changes are made and need to be amended as part of the redrafting work. It should also be apparent when the change was made (eg by date entries on the document list and by dating the revised pages of the document). This becomes important in audits; when examining records arising from a procedure it may well be important to know which version of the procedure applied at the date a record was taken.

It is also good practice (and more or less required by the Standard) to ensure that the specific changes in the document are highlighted in some way. Anyone reading and following a procedure etc can then quickly see what is new. Highlighting can be achieved in various ways; the most common is to mark the margin of the text with a vertical line (if the change has removed text this can be signified by a line against blank spacing). Only the most recent changes are identified in this way and when the document is redrafted, any previous change markings are removed. Obviously, whatever convention is used to highlight changes, staff using the documents need to understand what these are, eg as part of general training in use of the quality system.

Once redrafted, the required number of copies of the document are printed. This required number will be equal to the number of approved copies in circulation of the original version plus one for record purposes (see shortly). Except in very large organisations, the printing volume is likely to be modest and can normally be done on the in-house photocopier. If controlled documents are printed on special paper, the quality manager needs to ensure that there are sufficient stocks available. Other methods in use to make controlled documents visually distinctive include stamping each page 'controlled document'; most quality managers will want to delegate this task (but must make sure that all the pages are stamped).

In a smaller organisation, distribution of the revised documents may amount to no more than the quality manager (or someone to whom the task is delegated) going to each set of procedures etc and substituting the new version for the old (which is then destroyed except for any sets kept for record purposes). This will be impractical in larger organisations, particularly where there are several scattered sites. In such cases the quality manager will have to rely on others to make the changes; the new versions can be sent to each keeper of controlled document sets with an instruction to replace the superseded version. It is recommended that some positive evidence that this has been done should be required – eg a signed form or the return of replaced and superseded versions (this should ensure they do not stay 'in use'). However it is done, the changes need to be completed in a defined period or by a certain date; there can then be some confidence about when the change actually came into effect.

A change in procedures may entail a redesign of a form used to record quality data and sometimes the change is only an amendment of such a form. Copies of the new form will of course go with the controlled sets of procedures but others are needed for day-to-day use. These also need to be distributed and, equally importantly, the superseded versions removed. Ensuring this happens and that old forms are not left around is not easy and needs careful planning as well as the involvement of staff and line management. The need to use the new forms should be included in notices or training about the changes (see shortly).

Procedures and other controlled documents do not have to be in hard copy. The modern equivalent is for access on screen via a computer network. Where this is practical (ie in organisations which are well computerised for other reasons and where virtually all staff can practically access the network), most of the problems of revision and document control are solved automatically. Amendment of the computer files containing the quality system procedures is strictly controlled (it has to be), but once the change has been made, all users will have immediate access to the revised version via the network and the old version simply goes off the system.

RECORDING CHANGES

If not essential, it is useful and good practice to keep a running record of all changes made to a quality system. Keeping such a record enables system changes and the detail of the changes to be checked, for example by internal auditors and outside assessors. A record of past versions is also useful when considering future changes, otherwise there is some danger that past mistakes in procedures will be unintentionally repeated. Also keeping a record takes very little effort.

The only principle to observe in keeping change records is to ensure that copies of superseded documents are not mistaken for current versions; they are not in any sense 'in use'. In most cases this can be best achieved by the quality manager keeping the only copies of the replaced documents. They should be in a particular place and identified (eg by a line through each page). Each set of superseded documents can be bound in a looseleaf file together with a copy of the new version which replaced them (arguably these should also be identified as record copies). If, as we recommended, all changes are authorised through the corrective action process, the relevant corrective action reference can also be appended to the revised or superseded document versions. As time goes on, the archives generated in this way are likely to become quite substantial and some form of indexing will be needed.

LETTING EVERYONE KNOW

In theory, staff should learn of any revisions made to a quality system simply through their regular reference to the documents. In practice this does not work. Whatever might be desirable, most staff do not read procedures. This is not to say they do not follow them; they may learn what is required in other ways, including any quality system training that is provided. Something more, therefore, is needed to make staff aware of changes in the quality system.

The minimum required is to circulate or display a brief notice highlighting the change. This should identify the parts of the system which have changed (by reference number) and urge everyone to read the revisions. A short summary or abstract of the changes can also be included but this has some dangers – staff will often not read more than this summary and miss the detail that is required.

Beyond drawing attention to the changes by means such as notices etc, training is often needed as well for all but the most superficial changes. The quality manager can organise and run these sessions or have other managers do it (in which case they must discuss the changes with the quality manager). The degree of formality in such training will depend on the extent and nature of the changes made. See also Chapter 5 for further discussion of training.

AUDITING CHANGES

The final step in the change process is to assess whether or not the new procedures (or other parts of the quality system) are working effectively. This is done through the audit process discussed in Chapter 7.

If the change originated in an audit finding (ie a corrective action was raised as a result of an audit), its effectiveness will be established through the follow-up audit procedure which concentrates on whether the corrective action raised in the original audit has been dealt with effectively – ie 'closed out'. Where the change was initiated in some other way than an initial audit, its effectiveness should be established in the next scheduled audit in the area concerned. In preparing their checklist, auditors should check what changes have been made in procedures applicable to the particular area since the last audit and make a special effort to check these. If necessary, the quality manager may need to have an unscheduled audit carried out, eg if the likely effectiveness of the new procedure is contentious or if otherwise too long would elapse before the next scheduled audit is due.

15

DEALING WITH ASSESSORS

Gaining ISO 9000 registration should not be all that is sought from a quality system. However, for most organisations it will be an important goal and this chapter discusses assessment, the process of gaining registration to the Standard. The quality manager will be the point of contact between the organisation and assessors and have responsibility for making all the practical arrangements involved.

The relevance of this chapter will depend on when the reader becomes involved in a quality system. If registration has already been achieved, at least the earlier parts of the chapter will already be familiar through practical experience. However, as in other parts of the book, we shall assume that the starting point is a system about to be implemented and, therefore, assessment is still to come.

CHOOSING ASSESSORS

Anyone can set themselves up as ISO 9000 assessors and 'award' the Standard. Whether a certificate from the Easy Pass Global Certification Body will impress anybody is a different matter. For achievement of ISO 9000 to be generally accepted and recognised, the assessment needs to be carried out by a body accredited by the NACCB (National Accreditation Council for Certification Bodies). The process of this accreditation ensures assessment bodies work to a common standard and that, therefore, registration through each body is of equal standing. NACCB* accreditation is not blanket but is given to cover assessment of specific types of organisations and activities – the 'scope' of accreditation – and in selecting an assessor, a first consideration is whether their scope covers your own organisation's activity; with now very few exceptions, nearly all activities are within the scope of one or more of the assessment bodies.

There are broadly two types of assessors to choose from: those specialising in one particular industry and those covering all or most activities. An example of the former is The Quality Scheme for Ready Mixed Concrete – well worth considering for a company in that industry but not otherwise. General assessment bodies include BSi QA, SGS Yarsley, NQA, Lloyds Register Quality Assurance, Det Norske Veritas Quality Assurance and others. A full and up-to-date list of all accredited assessment bodies can be obtained from the NACCB.

Assessors may be the 'examiners' who award or withhold ISO 9000, but they are also suppliers to the organisations using their services and should be selected using the same care as dealing with other providers of specialised services. In most cases there will be at least several potential assessors to consider and evaluate.

The process of selecting an assessor can start about the time the quality system is first implemented. Assessment will not be then imminent, but most bodies have a full programme of work and will need two or three months notice before the agreed date. Since the system needs to bed in (see later) this should cause no practical delay if an early initial approach is made.

We recommend writing to a number of assessment bodies which appear suitable, providing brief details of your organisation – size, activities and where you are up to in planning a quality system. The response will be some details of the service offered and a questionnaire for you to provide more detailed information. Those assessment bodies you then choose to follow up (ie send a formal application to) will then provide a quotation of the costs of their service and other details of the contract they offer (which may be for a period of up to three years). Depending on the size of your own organisation, the assessment body may also make a preliminary

---

* NACCB (National Accreditation Council for Certification Bodies), 19 Buckingham Gate, London SW1E 6LB. Tel: 0171-233 7111.

visit before providing a formal quotation. This can be a way of getting to know more about the service offered and a 'feel' for the assessors.

Assessment bodies operate by selling the services of their professional staff and their quotation will be based on their hourly charge-out rates and their estimate of the input required for the assessment. The size of the organisation to be assessed, its structure – particularly in terms of the number and spread of sites – and the complexity of the processes and the quality system will all affect the final costs. No averages can be realistically given. However, even a small firm is likely to pay £1,000 or more for initial assessment and a similar amount each year for follow-up surveillance visits (see below). Large organisations may have assessment costs in the tens of thousands of pounds.

Once the quotations have been received they can be compared and a choice made. Costs will vary and are certainly one factor to consider along with other terms including the contract length. However, how well you feel you can work with the assessment body is at least as important. Obviously this is not easy to judge in advance; taking references from their other clients, including any in your own industry, may help in the decision. Another consideration is their experience of your specific type of business. The accreditation scope categories are quite wide and you may wish to select on a finer basis than this. The initial choice does not commit you forever to the particular assessment body; as we discuss later you can change assessor after initial registration. However, to make a switch within two or three years can be expensive since the whole assessment and surveillance process may have to start from scratch again.

THE INITIAL ASSESSMENT PROCESS

Desk Investigation

Assessment to ISO 9000 is in two distinct stages: a desk investigation and an on-site assessment. The desk investigation is carried out well before the on-site assessment and the objective is to establish whether the documented quality system meets the requirements of the Standard. Whether the quality system is being followed is not at this point a concern of the assessors. The specific arrangements for desk investigation vary between assessment bodies; some examine the documented system during an initial visit while others require the manuals etc to be sent to them. Either way, however, the focus is exclusively on whether everything required by ISO 9000 has been adequately covered in the system. If there are considered to be any gaps in this respect, the problem needs solving before the site assessment; the system must be changed so that it does meet the requirements of the Standard, and if necessary the on-site assessment date may need to be put back. Even if no major gaps are seen, the outcome from the desk investigation is usually some comments and observations which may need to be considered and changes made. However, some of the issues raised may not be black and white and there is room for discussion and argument with the assessors on the details of the system. The quality manager should contact the assessor to discuss such matters rather than rush to make changes which appear to be of doubtful value.

Between the desk investigation and the next stage, several weeks may elapse. During this time there is no reason to delay any changes to the system which are required as a result of internal audits or other reasons (including those required or suggested by the assessors); any such changes will be checked early in the on-site assessment.

On-site Assessment

Once the desk investigation is concluded (ie the assessor accepts that the system meets the Standard) the process moves to the on-site assessment. Now at issue is not whether the system meets the Standard but whether it is being followed. Compliance with each part of the system, and especially the procedures, is assessed, using the same methods which should be by now familiar through internal audit work – observing staff in their work, asking them questions and checking the evidence of records and particularly the latter. Time is also spent in discussions with the quality manager and the parts of the system normally covered first are those which most directly concern him or her – internal audits, corrective actions, management review and similar areas. How long all this takes will depend on the size and structure of the organisation, the complexity of its processes and system and how many staff are allocated to the assessment work. A one-site service industry company, employing 50, may require, for example, a two-day assessment by a single assessor.

The outlook of assessors is positive; they are looking for evidence that the system is being followed – they must meet NACCB standards in their work but they prefer to be able to award ISO 9000 than not. However, like internal auditors, assessors may well find evidence that the system is not being followed completely. Any such nonconformities identified will be classified as either minor or major.

Minor nonconformities are those where a procedure is not being followed in every case examined – the assessor looks at the records associated with a process and finds that, say, one in three is not completed as it ought to be (ie as specified in the system). The intention to follow the system is perhaps evident but there are some omissions of detail. In virtually all assessments, some such minor nonconformities will be found and providing there are not too many (but 'too many' cannot be defined) ISO 9000 can still be awarded. This is, however, conditional on the minor nonconformities being addressed and a solution sought as soon as possible; certainly by the time of the first surveillance visit (see shortly).

Major nonconformities are a different matter. These are cases where a significant part of the system is not being followed at all – in the process referred to above, for example, no records at all are being kept. Also a number of minor nonconformities with a common theme may be regarded as amounting to a major nonconformity; an example might be that the standard of record-keeping across several processes or throughout the system was found to be poor. If a major nonconformity is found, the ISO 9000 certificate cannot be awarded and a follow-up reassessment will be required. This may be on the scale of the first assessment or concentrate on the area of specific deficiency. It all depends on how bad things were found to be. Either way extra charges will of course be made by the assessment body.

It should be encouraging that the large majority of organisations get through the assessment at the first attempt – nor should this be surprising. Any mismatch of the system to the Standard should have been identified and put right after the desk investigation and all that can go wrong then is that the organisation fails to follow its own system. A company seriously implementing a quality system will be carrying out regular internal auditing to check compliance and any major nonconformity should have been identified and solved well before the assessment visit. If a major nonconformity is found on assessment, the internal auditing process has not been carried out effectively or else any problems identified have not been dealt with. Either way, the quality manager may have to accept some of the blame.

Awarding the Certificate

If all goes well (ie no worse than minor nonconformities are raised) the assessor will normally indicate that the assessment is successful and that an ISO 9000 registration is likely to be awarded. There is, though, a formality for the assessment body to go through and there is likely to be a couple of weeks delay before it is all official and the success can be publicised – in the meantime, internal celebrations are appropriate and the quality manager should make sure that all staff are aware of their success.

This then is the initial assessment process. How should an organisation prepare itself to ensure that all goes well?

PREPARING FOR ASSESSMENT

Between the start-up of the system and the on-site assessment, bedding-in is needed (the desk investigation will probably be carried out during this intervening period). This is so that experience of running the system is gained and the inevitable initial problems of faulty system design are solved. Time is also needed to build up sufficient quality records; these are largely the basis of the assessment and a number of them are needed for a realistic assessment of whether the system is being followed. How long is needed for this bedding-in? A lot will depend on the organisation and its processes. For example, other things being equal, a company with a process cycle of less than a day (eg a delivery service) will require a shorter period than one with a cycle of several months (eg plant manufac-turers, those carrying out major consultancy projects, etc). However, the minimum bedding-in time required is likely to be not less than three months (some assessors will not carry out an on-site assessment until the system has been in operation for this period at least), while anything over twelve months is, arguably, rather long – if the quality system is not working well by then there is something seriously wrong with it. What is not a valid reason for delaying assessment is that the staff 'have not got the time to work the system properly'. This excuse is sometimes made but it reflects totally the wrong attitude. If the staff have not got the time to work the quality system why have it at all? Possibly lack of time may be a good reason for delaying the start-up of a system but once it is implemented it must be followed with real commitment. A quality system that is half-hearted is not worth having at all. If this problem exists, the quality manager needs to change attitudes fundamentally or question why he or she is doing the job.

As already mentioned (Chapter 7), but worth repeating, is the need for internal auditing between start-up and assessment. The aim should be to audit the entire system in this period. This should not only ensure that any major problems are found and solved before assessment but it also prepares staff for the assessment visit; if they are doing their job in the right way, internal auditors will carry out the work in much the same way as outside assessors – possibly they may well be rather stricter.

Pre-assessment

Before the full assessment, some organisations like to have a dummy run – a pre-assessment. This involves outsiders coming in, wearing an assessor's hat, and examining the system and its workings as though they were carrying out a full initial assessment (although they may not, for cost reasons, aim to cover the whole system). Any weaknesses are, in this way, found and put right before the assessment. Also the pre-assessment can have a more diagnostic element. At the real thing, assessors may give some advice but strictly speaking this is outside the role of an assessor. Possibly, therefore, although an assessor may raise a nonconformity during the full assessment, he or she is not bound to give advice on how to put matters right and may well choose not to do so for all sorts of reasons. A problem found in a pre-assessment on the other hand would be followed by some advice.

Pre-assessment service can be bought from various sources including quality consultants such as those who advised on the development of the system (although in this case a different individual should do the pre-assessment to ensure the necessary independence of view). However, the assessment bodies also offer this service as well and there are some obvious reasons for choosing them – while assessors all work to the

197

NACCB standard there are some variations in style and it is an advantage to gain experience of the approach in a pre-assessment.

There is much to recommend pre-assessment and the only argument against it is its cost. The charge rates from assessment bodies are much the same as for final assessment although the input (and therefore the full cost) is typically less. One argument against pre-assessment is that if the cost is a significant proportion of full assessment why not take the risk anyway since even if further assessment is needed (because of a problem) the total costs may not be much more. Against this view is that it ignores the value of any diagnostic advice given during pre-assessment and that failure in the full assessment is bad for morale and the risks of it happening should be minimised. Another view is that the money for pre-assessment might be better spent on internal auditor training – the benefits are more permanent and well trained auditors should also be able to adequately test the system.

Beyond bedding-in, carrying out frequent and thorough audits and possibly having a pre-assessment, there is little more that can be done to prepare an organisation and its staff for assessment. Basically the system is working or it is not. Arguably it is better not to get staff over-nervous for assessment day; all they need to do is answer any questions asked by assessors to the best of their ability and if they do not know to say so. Obviously on assessment day the relevant staff need to be available. This does not have to mean everyone but certainly most of the management; the quality manager should know whose presence is likely to be vital. The audit process is always of particular interest to assessors and the auditors should be available. Where more than one site is involved, the assessor can be expected to indicate when they wish to visit each one; if there are many branches, a sample rather than all may be covered and a timetable should be indicated before-hand.

More than anyone else, the quality manager will be involved with the assessors. He or she will liaise with them in all arrangements, deal with issues arising from the desk investigation and probably accompany them throughout the on-site assessment (including to see where and why any problems are found). The quality manager is in all senses the point of contact between the organisation and the assessors.

SURVEILLANCE AND REASSESSMENT

Gaining ISO 9000 is not like passing a driving test; even when you have the certificate and registration that is not the end of the assessment process. Assessment has to be ongoing if ISO 9000 registration is to be kept. The assessors will return for surveillance visits and possibly a full reassessment.

In one sense ongoing assessment is a nuisance; it all takes up the quality manager's time, disturbs many other staff and costs money as well – the assessment body's contract will include charges for this follow-up. However, it should be clear that ongoing assessment is needed if registration and certification is to be worth anything. Without this process, an organisation with the wrong outlook could simply work a quality system until successful at the first assessment and then let it lapse. Another argument is that even those committed to quality and a quality system need that little extra push to comply, especially when things are hectic. The certainty of surveillance visits is an additional reason to make the system work well all the time.

Surveillance visits are made at six-monthly intervals. In principle they are carried out in the same way as the initial assessment but only part rather than all the system will be covered and the process will take less time (eg one man-day rather than two or three). Also, like the initial assessment, minor or even major nonconformities will be raised if problems are found. Minor nonconformities should be dealt with before the next visit – the same as in the initial assessment. Major nonconformities must also be addressed and may be followed up in an extra (charged for) visit. They can result in removal of certification (loss of ISO 9000) although this would be very unlikely as an outcome of a single surveillance visit (but very likely if the problem was not quickly dealt with after that). Certification will also of course be lost if the contract with the assessment body lapses, ie the organisation decides to have no more surveillance visits.

The assessment bodies vary in their policy on reassessment. Some may insist that after three years the whole assessment process is started again with a repeat full assessment carried out in exactly the same way as the initial assessment. Others, however, normally continue with surveillance visits indefinitely and do not require full reassessment unless there is a fundamental change in the operation covered by the ISO 9000 registration.

Differences in policy in this respect affect long-term costs since the charges for assessment are higher than for surveillance – an assessor requiring reassessment may be cheaper over three years than another not requiring this but over four years their relative costs may be reversed. Policies in respect of reassessment may well be a factor which influences the initial choice.

Where reassessment is the policy, the assessor's contract period will tie in with this cycle and when reassessment is due, another assessment body can be considered without any additional assessment costs being incurred. The quality manager, at this juncture, probably ought to at least consider alternatives and both costs and the service provided can be re-evaluated. The position is rather different in the case of assessors with a continuous surveillance policy. Depending on the contract terms, an alternative assessor body can be considered at any time but if a change is made the new assessor may require to carry out and charge for some initial assessment. In this sense assessment is not fully transferable and this is some barrier to change. Also if the ISO 9000 assessment logo is used on publicity material (see below) this will have to be changed with the switch of assessor. This too has a cost (which is also borne in the case of a change made on reassessment).

During surveillance visits, assessors may make suggestions and observations on improvements to the quality system over and above anything needed to deal with nonconformities. Some bodies claim that their friendly and positive approach in this respect is an added value of the service offered to clients. One area where advice will certainly be given is when there is a revision in the Standard. When this happens, the assessment bodies will give advice to their certificate holders in the form of documents describing the implications of the revisions and what might be practically required. They may also offer low-cost seminars which quality managers can attend to discuss what is involved. On the basis of this advice, or otherwise, the registered organisation is expected to make any changes in their system required to bring it into line with the revised Standard. The extent to which this has been done will be checked at the next surveillance visit following publication of the revised standard. If the necessary changes have not been made, nonconformities will be raised and action required by the time of the next surveillance visit. Advice on how to deal with the specific deficiencies will probably be given as well.

MARKETING ISO 9000

Having gone to all the trouble of gaining ISO 9000 it is well worth marketing this achievement regardless of whether impressing potential customers was a major reason for the project. What we have in mind is no more than using ISO 9000 registration as a means of communicating a commitment to quality and the benefits this offers customers.

There are many tools to use in such marketing – the correct ones depend on the market concerned and available budgets. Since planning a marketing strategy and tactics are outside most quality manager's responsibilities and expertise, it will not be discussed in any detail here. However, the quality manager should at least push others to do something positive. He or she should also advise on the use (and warn against the misuse) of the ISO 9000 logo.

Every assessment body has its own ISO 9000 logo (an example is shown in Figure 15.1) which successfully assessed organisations are entitled to use in their own publicity if they wish. The right to this logo has a value since it confirms that the Standard has been attained and distinguishes the organisation from those (too many) who make dubious claims in this respect (eg 'working to ISO 9000').

Figure 15.1   Example of assessment body's ISO 9000 logo

This logo can be used in a wide range of ways including on letterheads, in brochures, on copies of the quality policy (which might be used as a publicity mailing), on delivery vehicles, on flags and on buildings. Each assessment body will provide artwork for the logo and also advise on how it can and cannot be used – any misuse, including by those not entitled to it because they are not currently assessed, will be pursued. If an organisation loses its registration it must cease using the logo and, as already mentioned, it must change the logo if a switch is made to a new supplier.

One way in which an ISO 9000 logo cannot be used is to make a claim about *product* quality, nor should this be implied in any other way which relates to this standard. Firms which claim their windows or computers or other products are 'made to ISO 9000' are consciously or otherwise misleading the market-place. ISO 9000 is a standard for quality management and implies nothing about the technical standards of the product. If this is not clear please reread Chapter 2.

16

BEYOND THE QUALITY SYSTEM

We have now covered the quality manager's responsibilities for an effective quality system. Once it is all in place, apparently working well and ISO 9000 achieved, is that all? Is it now just a matter of making sure it all ticks over? We think not – there is more to gain from a quality system than just operating it well enough to meet the Standard. Also, the whole quality process can be taken further still, into what is commonly called total quality management or TQM. In previous chapters we have tried to give practical advice on how to be an effective quality manger. There is not much that is practical in this final chapter but we hope there is something to inspire.

MAKING THE QUALITY SYSTEM REALLY WORK

In much of this book, the emphasis has been on the various mechanisms a quality manager needs in place to operate an effective quality system. We described and discussed activities such as internal auditing, monitoring various sorts of nonconformity, corrective actions, controlling and changing the documentation, management reviews and working with the assessors. The quality manager is closely involved in all of this and must learn how to operate what may, initially, seem strange and unfamiliar processes. This sort of active management of the quality system is essential if even minimal benefits are going to be obtained. The quality manager's routine activities are, therefore, essential and valuable. In time, however, the mechanisms making up the system will all become second nature and at this point some quality managers may be tempted to settle down to a quiet life, making sure it all runs to routine, perhaps from time to time making sure corrective actions are raised (it will keep staff on their toes) and if a real crisis happens putting some energy into that. Even in this case, the organisation is almost certainly better off than before a quality system was brought in and the quality manager is probably earning his or her keep. However, a lot more can be done with the quality system than this.

Although much of the book has been about routines and administration, as we discussed in Chapter 4 a really effective quality manager is more than an administrator, and the most important role on top of 'housekeeping' is championing the system and quality generally. This means keeping and raising the level of commitment throughout the organisation, among fellow managers but equally among all staff. This includes getting a high level of involvement in quality issues and in using the system. Continuously, the quality manager should stress that the quality system is there to *use* – to solve problems, to stop them happening again and, in the end, to raise continuously quality sights and make real improvements. Some would argue that ISO 9000 is more about maintaining quality standards than raising them but an effective system, backed by commitment, inevitably leads to improvement. In particular, the quality triangle of internal auditing, corrective action and management review, providing it is all more than a matter of form, must lead to positive change and quality enhancement.

Even if improvement is seen as the results of other sorts of activities, the quality system is still involved because it makes sure the rest of the processes continue to work effectively while change is considered and introduced in a particular area. As Figure 16.1 indicates, quality can be thought of as a slope which the organisation needs to keep climbing. It also, however, needs to make sure that it does not start to slip backwards while concentrating on exciting prospects for change and improvement ahead. In this sense the quality system is the safety chock. The quality manager therefore needs both to keep the chock sound (routine administration of the quality system) and at the same time look up the quality slope to see where the organisation should be moving. The quality manager is also likely to be the main 'pusher' up the slope, motivating improvement.

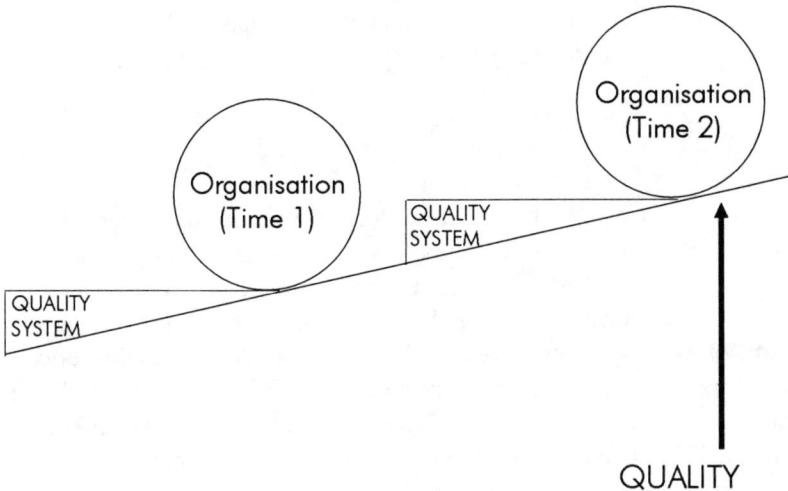

Figure 16.1 The quality slope

As the organisation moves up the quality slope, the quality system will need to change. We have emphasised the need for this change (Chapter 14) and the quality manager's role in controlling this. The various mechanisms (internal auditing, corrective action, etc) will identify where parts of the system need changing but beyond this the quality manager (preferably also involving other managers) needs to take a more global view and from time to time think about whether the system continues to meet the organisation's needs. Procedures in particular have a tendency to endure, despite changes in the situations they are meant to cover.* Periodically they need reviewing to see if they are still valid. If a procedure (or other

---

* It is said that during the Second World War it was found that anti-aircraft batteries appeared to have one too many crew. The extra man appeared to be there to 'hold the horse's head when the gun fired'.

part of a quality system) does not serve any real and practical purpose it should be changed – if it is not worth doing, do not do it. In particular, never let the quality system stand in the way of achieving quality – meeting customer requirements. If a procedure stops an organisation responding effectively to a customer there is something wrong with it – to tell a customer that you cannot meet a requirement 'because of ISO 9000' (this is not uncommon) defeats the whole point of quality assurance.

TQM

TQM is often thought of as a next step up from quality systems and a quality manager with an effective system in place can usefully think about some of the techniques involved. Compared to quality systems and the ISO 9000 approach, TQM is rather vaguer. It covers many techniques, some of which are alternatives to others in the bundle. In part this reflects the different TQM gurus with their own emphases and agendas. What these are must be found in another source; we make no claim to this being another TQM book. What can be said is that all the techniques can work sometimes and in some organisations but you have to pick and choose those which are most likely to take root. We will limit ourselves to commenting on four areas of TQM which are natural outgrowths from a quality system approach. These are extending the scope of quality, getting closer to customers, people empowerment and quality as a journey rather than a goal.

Extending the Scope of Quality

A quality system developed to meet ISO 9000 does not have to cover all the operations of an organisation; some activities are outside the specific requirements of ISO 9000 and this includes accounts and finance, various aspects of company management and much of marketing and sales (only 'contract review' is formally covered by the Standard). This is illustrated in Figure 16.2.

However, if a quality system approach proves to be beneficial in the areas that must be covered to meet ISO 9000 why not extend it to cover all the organisation? One way or another the whole organisation is

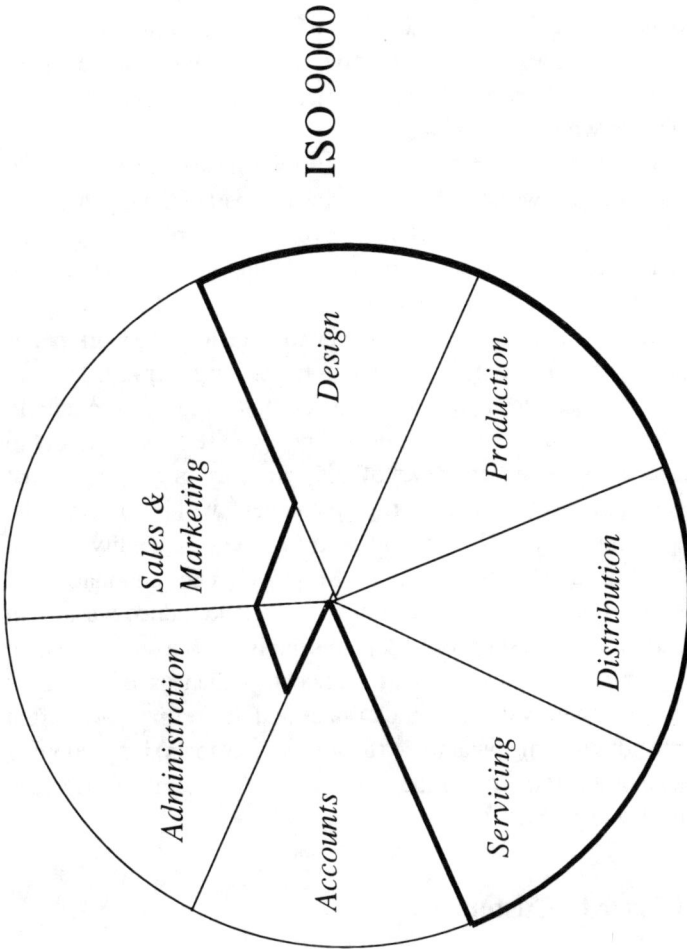

Figure 16.2 The limited coverage of ISO 9000 systems

involved in quality and meeting requirements – this is one of the insights of TQM. One argument against doing this is that it will expose more of the operation to outside assessors. Arguably, though, this is not true; if the assessment is against ISO 9000, assessors generally do not stray into areas where there is no specific requirement in the Standard. Even so, is it such a bad thing to be assessed? An effective system should stand up to assessment and if it does not there is something wrong with it. A bad system is always worse than no system.

Of the main 'outside' areas, accounts and finance always need a systematic approach to work at all and to bring this part of the organisation into the formal system almost certainly involves little more than documenting what is already in place. Moreover, accounts do have an interface with customers and the satisfaction of their requirements. Integrating the department into quality management will encourage them to work better in this respect. The same can be said for administration generally. The real battleground may be sales and marketing. Of course they are crucially involved in meeting customer requirements but even so they are likely to be the least receptive to systems. Part of this reluctance may be a fear that their skills and flair, so essential to bring in business, will in some way be lessened and constrained. This should be a false fear; a quality system should not and need not stifle creativity. Moreover, sales and marketing are often areas of activity which cry out for efforts to reduce waste – in this case mainly valuable staff time spent ineffectively. If a quality system can reduce scrap in production and reduce the chances of mistakes recurring, it can certainly do the same in sales and marketing where often the answer to not knowing what to do (to achieve the goals) is to redouble the effort – having lost their way they run harder. A system approach can start to solve these problems.

Getting Closer to Customers

This brings us to the second area of TQM we plan to discuss: getting closer to customers. Apart from reviewing contracts, perhaps understanding their design requirements and dealing with any complaints, ISO 9000 requires little else in relation to the principal partner in a quality relationship. However, as we argued in Chapter 10, with quite a small effort the system can be expanded to cover customer monitoring and this will help to improve the ability to meet customer requirements and stop any dissatisfactions festering into real complaints or a switch to other suppliers. But the focus here is still on customers' present requirements. What of their future needs of which even they may as yet be uncertain? The TQM answer here is to do as much as possible to get close to customers. This may involve formal market research, extensive visits to customers' sites and staff exchanges, but may also mean refocusing all departments to be involved in customer satisfaction. The effect of all this is to dissolve the barriers and boundaries between the customer and the organisation.

A practical step in relation to the customer interface is to promote a customer satisfaction culture within the organisation. The concept of the internal customer can work here. Whatever high sounding words may be said and however the organisation may change, many staff inevitably have little contact with real, outside customers. However, they all take part in processes which involve receiving an input from one part of the organisation and, after carrying out the process, passing the ouput on to another department or group of staff. The source of the input is an internal supplier and where it goes after processing is an internal customer. Everyone is, therefore, both an internal supplier and customer. Suppliers and customers need to work closely together to define, meet and anticipate all requirements.

People Empowerment

This leads to the principle that the only source of quality improvement is the people who make it all happen: the staff of the organisation. The more staff who are involved in quality activities and the more they are empowered to make improvements, the greater the benefits will be. If, on the other hand, staff believe that quality is for someone else, for sales, for management or for the boss, the less the progress. Throughout this book, we have argued for involvement in the processes of the quality system and this is a form of the empowerment preached by TQM. Other forms include the likes of quality circles to generate and harness innovatory improvements. Linked to this is that TQM is about hearts and minds and, therefore, very much a people-centred approach – more so than quality systems and ISO 9000. However, it is more a matter of emphasis than a fundamental difference. Also in this context, beware of playing at TQM. Attitudes are very hard to change and a few meetings to raise quality consciousness by saying fine words, launching a few gimmicks, etc, will have a transient impact, if any at all. TQM cannot be 'done' like this. Beautiful thoughts may be worth having, but quality is about *doing* things, not just saying them.

Quality is a Journey

And so to the final point. Developing a quality system was hopefully all worthwhile. So is the quality manager's work in ensuring it is implemented successfully and works well. Going further and bringing in TQM techniques may also bring benefits. But at no one point has quality been finally achieved. Quality levels can be improved but never to a point where they cannot be surpassed since, even if you do everything that is possible with a process, the requirements and the environment in which you meet them will change. Quality is, therefore, not a goal to be attained but a journey to follow and one that will never end.

BIBLIOGRAPHY

Asher, J M (1992) *Implementing TQM in Small and Medium Sized Companies*, Technical Communications, Letchworth.

Dale, B and Oakland, J S (1991) *Quality Improvement Through Standards*, Stanley Thornes, Leckhampton.

Jackson, P and Ashton, D (1993) *Implementing Quality Through BS 5750 (ISO 9000)*, Kogan Page, London.

Jackson, P and Ashton, D (1995) *Achieving ISO 9000 (BS 5750), An Introduction to Quality Registration*, Kogan Page, London.

Oakland, J (1989) *Total Quality Management*, Butterworth-Heinemann, Oxford.

Price, F (1984) *Right First Time*, Wildwood House, Aldershot.

Taguchi, G (1986) *Introduction to Quality Engineering*, UNIPUB/Kraus International, White Plains, New York.

Warwood, S J (1993) *The Role of the Modern Quality Manager*, Technical Communications, Letchworth.

INDEX